W   cts

       ists

Library of Congress Cataloging-in-Publication Data
Carson, Mary Kay.
    Weather projects for young scientists : experiments and science fair ideas / Mary Kay
Carson.
      p. cm.
    Includes index.
    ISBN-13: 978-1-55652-629-9
    ISBN-10: 1-55652-629-6
  1. Weather—Experiments—Juvenile literature. 2. Science projects—Juvenile literature.
I. Title.
    QC981.3.C372 2007
    551.5078—dc22

                                                                        2006016430

Cover design: Joan Sommers
Interior design: Scott Rattray
Interior illustrations: Gail Rattray

Photo Credits
Front cover images: top and lower left courtesy of Tom Uhlman; center left (wea00415)
courtesy of National Oceanic and Atmospheric Administration (NOAA) Photo Library;
center right (nssl0054) courtesy of NOAA Photo Library, NOAA Central Library;
OAR/ERL/National Severe Storms Laboratory (NSSL); lower right courtesy of
NASA/Jeff Schmaltz, MODIS Land Rapid Response Team
Interior images
page 2 (STS-052-15-007) courtesy of NASA Johnson Space Center
page 13 courtesy NASA/Jeff Schmaltz, MODIS Land Rapid Response Team
pages 15 (wea00415), 18 (fly00102), 111 (spac0273) courtesy of National Oceanic and
    Atmospheric Administration (NOAA) Photo Library
page 19 (GL-2002-002528) courtesy of NASA Goddard Space Flight Center
pages 24, 40, 52, 56, 61, 69, 72, 88, 94, 99, 113, 119, 123 courtesy of Tom Uhlman
page 27 (line1486) courtesy of Sean Linehan, NOAA, NGS, Remote Sensing
page 43 (ISS004-E-12798) courtesy of NASA Johnson Space Center-Earth Sciences and
    Image Analysis
page 45 (corp1572) courtesy of Commander John Bortniak, NOAA Corps
page 50 (corp2395) courtesy of Michael Van Woert, NOAA NESDIS, ORA
pages 75 (nssl0010), 100 (nssl0028), 103 (nssl0054), 117 (nssl0027), courtesy of NOAA
    Photo Library, NOAA Central Library; OAR/ERL/National Severe Storms
    Laboratory (NSSL)
page 79 (line0687) courtesy of Mary Hollinger, NODC biologist, NOAA
pages 110 (noaa0908), 115 (noaa0911) courtesy of National Weather Service Headquarters
page 125 (PIA01526) courtesy of NASA Jet Propulsion Laboratory

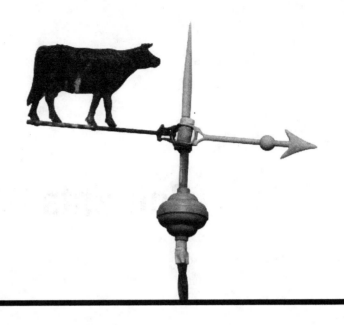

Weather Projects

for Young Scientists

Experiments and
Science Fair Ideas

MARY KAY CARSON

CHICAGO
REVIEW
PRESS

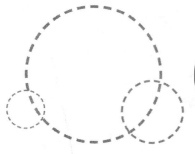

Contents

Acknowledgments

This book would not exist without the encouragement of editor Jerome Pohlen. Thanks also to Lisa Reardon for her work polishing the manuscript. Photographer Tom Uhlman deserves special thanks for contributing his always-amazing photographs. And much appreciation goes to the photo libraries of the National Oceanic and Atmospheric Administration (NOAA) and the National Aeronautics and Space Administration (NASA).

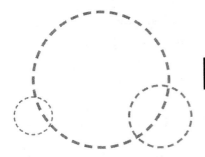

Introduction

What is weather? Weather is the condition of the air in a particular place at a specific time. The heat, pressure, and moisture in the air mix and churn to make the weather sunny, cloudy, windy, stormy, or clear. Weather is often confused with climate. But they're not the same thing. Climate is a region's regular pattern of weather over a long period of time. The climate in Hawaii may be tropical, but today's weather in Honolulu might be cool and dry. While weather often changes from day to day, a region's climate changes little over the centuries.

The weather information and activities in this book will help you discover all about wind and seasons, clouds and snow, storms of all sorts, and even weather-related careers. You'll learn about weather-measuring instruments and how to make your own in activities labeled Build a Weather Station. Look for the special activities and information sections marked Storm Science to find out more about hurricanes, tornadoes, lightning, snowstorms, and monsoons. There are also activities and information related to current environmental problems connected to weather. Just look for the Weather and the Environment label. Find out about Cool Weather Careers by reading these profiles of people working in weather-related jobs. You can take the activities in this book further, designing and doing your own experiments for fun—or as school projects. Look for the Science Fair Spin label for ideas to get you started. Key terms are in bold upon their first appearance and are defined in the glossary at the end of the book. Lastly, make sure to check out the weather Web sites on page 131.

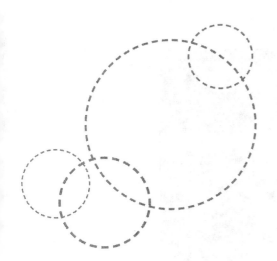

The Air Around Us

The earth is surrounded by a blanket of air called the **atmosphere**. Earth's air is mostly nitrogen and oxygen gas with small amounts of water vapor, carbon dioxide, and a few other trace gases. (See the pie chart at right.) The earth's gravitational pull anchors the atmosphere to the planet. Gravity keeps air from drifting off into outer space.

What's in Air?

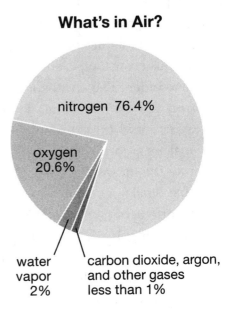

nitrogen 76.4%

oxygen 20.6%

water vapor 2%

carbon dioxide, argon, and other gases less than 1%

This photo taken by the space shuttle shows Earth's lower atmospheric layers lit by the setting sun. The bottom layer is the troposphere and the top, brighter layer is the stratosphere.

Layers of Air

Scientists divide the atmosphere into four main layers. (See diagram on page 3). The layer closest to the ground is the **troposphere**. It goes from the surface to about 7 miles (11 km) up. It has the most air and moisture of all the layers. It's where most weather happens. In this layer temperature decreases with height, so higher altitudes are colder. The **stratosphere** is from about 7 to 30 miles (11 to 48 km) above the ground. There is little mixing between the stratosphere and the troposphere, so hardly any water vapor and dust make it into the stratosphere. At the top of the stratosphere—and into the **mesosphere**—is the ozone layer, the band of O_3, or ozone, that blocks much of the sun's dangerous ultraviolet (UV) radiation from reaching the earth's surface. Ozone blocks UV radiation by absorbing it. While doing so, it also heats up the stratosphere, which is actually warmer at its top than at its bottom.

The mesosphere is from 30 to 50 miles (48 to 80 km) above the earth. The temperatures in this layer again begin to decrease with height, reaching as low as -90°F (-68°C). No commercial aircraft fly this high, only research weather balloons. The thermosphere is the layer from 50 to 180 miles (80 to 290 km) up, or more. After it is interplanetary space, or the exosphere. It gets super hot in the thermosphere, up to more than 3,000°F (1,650°C). The lower part of the thermosphere is also called the ionosphere and contains electrically charged particles or ions. Radio waves are reflected back to the earth by this layer. It's also where high-energy atomic particles from the sun collide with gases and produce beautiful streaks of colored light called auroras, or the northern lights.

The Atmosphere's Layers

Pressure mb (Pa)	Height mi (km)	Approx. Temp. of Layers °F (°C)	Layers of the Atmosphere
	36,000 (60,000)		
	3,600 (6,000)		
	360 (600)	2,200 (1,200)	thermosphere
10^{-8} (10^{-6})	180 (300)		ionosphere
0.01 (10)	53 (85)	-150 (-100)	
			mesosphere
			ozone layer
			stratosphere
250 (25,000)	7 (11)	-60 (-50)	troposphere
1,000 (100,000)	0	68 (20)	

Atmospheric Poster

You can make a great poster for your room of the layers of the atmosphere. Start by covering a section of a wall with paper or poster board. Use the information in The Atmosphere's Layers diagram on page 3 to help you draw the layers in correct proportions. If you have about 10 feet (3 meters) of wall height, use the scale of 1 cm = 1 km.

Once the layers are drawn and labeled, find out the characteristics of each atmospheric layer. Then write up an informational caption for each layer and paste it onto the poster inside the correct layer. Include the atmospheric layer's temperature, gases, atmospheric phenomena, and what human-made aircraft travel in that layer. You can also illustrate the layer with jets, space shuttles, meteorites, satellites, etc.

> **Fast Fact**
> The air around and above us—the atmosphere—weighs 11,000,000,000,000,000,000 pounds. (4,950,000,000,000,000,000 kg)

Create a three-dimensional diorama of the layers of the atmosphere.

Science Fair Spin

The Weight of Air

Air is invisible and may seem like it's made up of nothing at all. But the gases in air have weight and take up space. The weight of the air pushes on the earth's surface, just like a stack of blankets pushes down on a table. This pushing force is called **air pressure**. At sea level, air pressure is about 14.7 pounds per square inch (1 kg/cm^2). Air pressure lessens with height, however, halving about every 3.4

miles (5.5 km). There's less air pressure on top of a mountain than at sea level. We're literally living at the bottom of an ocean of air!

- -

Air Is Everywhere

Air may be made up of invisible gases, but it takes up space. Prove to yourself that air has volume in this activity.

You'll Need

- ► water
- ► funnel with a very narrow tip
- ► small clear plastic bottle (such as a salad dressing bottle)
- ► sharpened pencil
- ► modeling clay

1. Set the funnel inside the neck of the bottle. Think about what's filling up the inside of the "empty" bottle.

2. Pour water through the funnel until the bottle is halfway filled. Is there still air in the bottle? What happened to it?

3. Empty the water out of the bottle and replace the funnel.

4. Wrap a "collar" of modeling clay around the mouth of the bottle, so that it seals in the funnel. It needs to be airtight!

5. Try again to pour water through the funnel into the bottle. What happens? What's blocking the water from flowing in?

6. Now use the sharpened pencil to poke holes in the clay collar. What happens? How did the air that was trapped in the bottle escape?

Design an experiment that repeats this activity using funnels and bottles of different sizes and compare their results.

Science Fair Spin

- -

Balancing Balloons

Air may feel like nothing, but those gases do weigh something. Prove to yourself that air has mass in this activity. (Remember, weight is mass times gravity.)

You'll Need

- ▶ 2 identical balloons
- ▶ 4 four-inch (10-cm) strips of tape
- ▶ 2- to 3-foot-long (0.5–1 m) thin dowel or yardstick
- ▶ straight pin
- ▶ string
- ▶ friend to help

1. Blow up the balloons to equal sizes and tightly tie them closed.

2. Tape the balloons onto the ends of the dowel or yardstick using two equal-sized strips of tape on each balloon.

3. Tie the string loosely around the dowel or yardstick near its center. Hold the string away from your body and ask your friend to slide the string loop back and forth until the balloons balance.

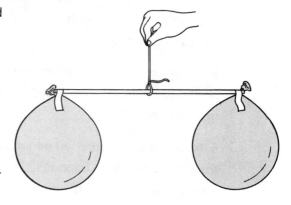

4. Continue to hold the balancing balloons by the string.

Have your friend CAREFULLY puncture one of the balloons with the straight pin by sticking it through a taped area. (This will keep the balloon from popping, the air will seep slowly out instead.)

5. What happened? Why are the balloons no longer balanced? What does the deflated balloon no longer have?

Pressure vs. Pencil

Anything that has weight and takes up space—like air—also exerts pressure. Living under the miles of atmosphere above us is like being under an ocean of air. Prove to yourself how air exerts pressure in this activity.

You'll Need
- ▶ unsharpened pencil
- ▶ 3 identical sheets of paper

1. Fold one sheet of paper in half and one into quarters. The third is left as is. Which of these papers weighs more?

2. Lay the pencil on the end of a desk or table so about 2 inches (5 cm) of it hangs over the edge. Set the quartered sheet of paper on top of the part of the pencil on the desk.

3. Tap the pencil with a quick, but gentle, downward stroke. What happens? Did you feel a lot of pressure pushing against the paper? Was it hard to flip the folded paper?

4. Repeat steps 2 and 3 with the halved paper. (Make sure you are tapping with the same strength.) What happens? Why did it feel harder to flip?

5. Repeat steps 2 and 3 with the open sheet of paper, again using equal force when tapping the pencil. What happens? What is keeping the paper "glued" to the desk? Why is there more air pressure pushing down on the unfolded sheet of paper

---

Highs and Lows

You already know there's more air pressure at sea level than on top of a mountain. But air pressure changes not only with height, but also with temperature. Warm air weighs less than cool air, so it rises. Warm air rises because its fast-moving molecules spread out, making warm air less dense and lighter than cool air.

Low Pressure System

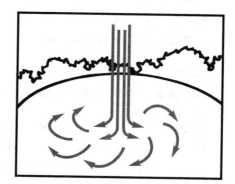

High Pressure System

An area of air that has a higher pressure than its surroundings is called a **high pressure system** or, or simply a *high*. The sinking air of a high pressure center dampens the upward movement of air needed for clouds to form. This is why an area of high pressure often brings clear weather. In contrast, a **low pressure system** (or *low*) has rising air, which encourages clouds to form and the rain or snow that comes from those clouds. Cloudy and rainy weather often result from an area of low pressure. The formation and movement of high and low pressure areas in the atmosphere drive much of the weather around the globe.

The Barometer

Air pressure is measured with an instrument called a **barometer**. (That's why air pressure is also called *barometric pressure*.) There are two basic kinds of barometers—the mercury barometer and the aneroid barometer. The mercury barometer was invented by an assistant of Galileo Galilee named Evangelista Torricelli in 1643. It's a simple instrument that has changed little since its invention. A mercury-filled tube that's closed at one end is placed upright with its open end down into a container of more mercury. Air pressure on the mercury in the container keeps the mercury from draining out of the tube. The more air pressure there is, the greater the pressure on the mercury in the container, and the higher the mercury in the tube is pushed up. A ruler set beside the tube is used to take measurements.

An aneroid barometer uses a flexible metal bellows instead of mercury to measure air pressure. The tiny accordion-like sealed cylinder shrinks and expands with changing air pressure. An attached pointer or pen indicates the amount of change on an attached scale.

Air pressure is measured in a number of different units. It can be measured in units of weight per unit of volume, like pounds per square inch or kilograms per square centimeter. However, the convention with American meteorologists is to refer to barometric pressure in simply "inches," which in fact means inches of mercury on a mercury barometer—even if the pressure was measured on a different kind of barometer. In other parts of the world air pressure is recorded in a standard metric measurement of pressure, called millibars. Yet another variation is the kilopascal, which is millibars divided by 10. An air pressure reading of 29.92 inches (of mercury) = 1013.25 millibars.

Mercury Barometer

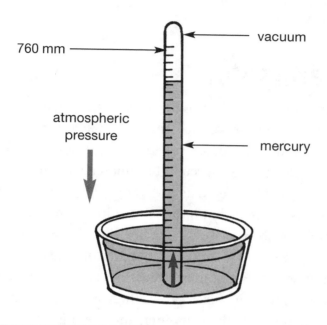

**Build a
Weather
Station**

Barometer

You can measure and track changes in atmospheric pressure with this easy-to-make barometer. It works like an aneroid barometer.

You'll Need

▶ empty coffee can or wide-mouthed jar
▶ large balloon
▶ duct tape
▶ toothpick
▶ clear tape
▶ 2 drinking straws
▶ scissors
▶ empty half-gallon jug or carton

1. Cut the neck off of a large balloon. Stretch the balloon top tightly over the can or jar. Use duct tape to secure it to the can or jar. It needs to be an airtight seal!

2. Attach two drinking straws together by pinching one and inserting it into the end of the other. They should overlap at least an inch. Tape the toothpick to one end of the combined straws so it sticks out a half inch or so (1 cm) from the end of the straws. This will be the barometer's indicator needle.

3. Lay the non-toothpick end of the combined straws on top of the balloon-covered can or jar. The end of the straws should be in the center of the balloon-covered top. Use a single strip of clear tape to attach the straw onto the balloon rubber.

4. Trace or photocopy the barometer scale below, or create your own.

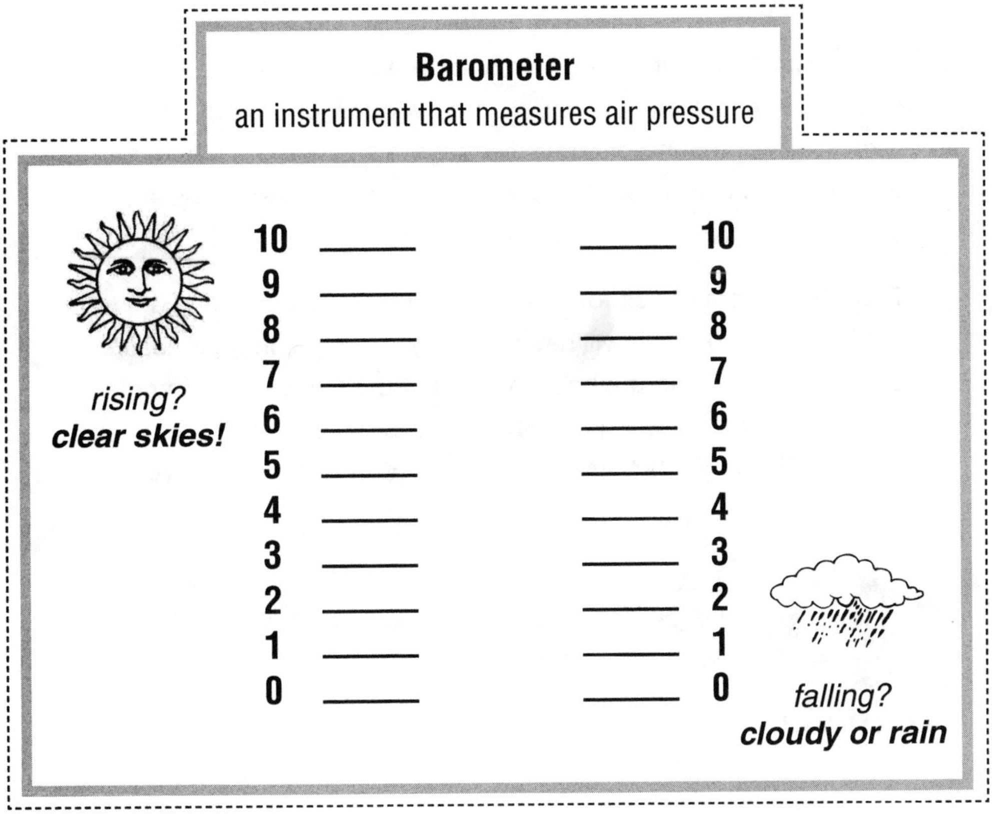

Barometer
an instrument that measures air pressure

rising?
clear skies!

10	10
9	9
8	8
7	7
6	6
5	5
4	4
3	3
2	2
1	1
0	0

falling?
cloudy or rain

5. Set the carton or jug behind the toothpick end of the straw. Tape the scale onto one side of the carton or jug.

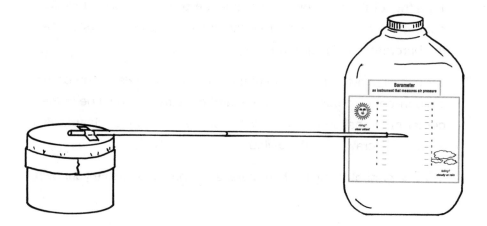

6. Set your barometer indoors in a still area where the temperature doesn't change. Don't set it in a sunny window or a drafty spot. (Note: This kind of barometer's readings are affected by temperature, which is why it must be kept in a temperature-stable place in order to get the most accurate readings.)

7. Let the barometer sit for a number of hours before taking a first reading. The toothpick will rise and fall as changes in air pressure contract and expand the balloon, moving the straw. You can create a chart with the following headings to record the air pressure over time: DATE, TIME, READING, WEATHER (Sunny, Cloudy, or Rainy?).

Design and build a barometer that works like a mercury barometer.

Science Fair Spin

Hurricane Katrina was one of the most destructive and deadly storms ever to hit the United States. This satellite image shows Katrina moving toward southern Louisiana.

Hurricanes

Hurricanes are the planet's largest storms. Hurricanes are usually 300 miles (480 km) in diameter and can have wind gusts in the 150 to 200 mph (240 to 320 km per hour) range. They start in the band of warm water near the equator when the ocean is at its warmest. (Hurricane season is June through November for North America and the Caribbean.)

Storm Science

Warm water of 80°F (27°C) or more is the needed fuel for these giant storms. The moisture from the warm water evaporates into the air hanging above it. This creates warm, moist, low-pressure rising air. As this air moves upward, it cools, and its water vapor condenses into clouds and rain. In order for water vapor to change to liquid water, a tremendous amount of heat must be released. This released heat in turn warms up the surrounding air, causing it to rise faster and create even lower pressure at the surface.

> **Fast Fact**
>
> The energy output of a single hurricane is equivalent to the amount of electricity used in the United States during six months!

Outlying higher-pressure air rushes into the new low-pressure area as fast-moving updrafts and eventually a huge whirling mass of air called a **tropical depression** can form. If the depression continues to be fueled by the engine of heat and low pressure of warm water, it's classified as a hurricane once its winds have reached 74 mph (119 km per hour).

A hurricane's strength is determined by just how low its pressure is. The lower the pressure, the faster and stronger outside air rushes in toward it, so the faster the winds. The low pressure also causes the sea level below the storm to rise, which becomes a flooding mound of water—called a storm surge—if the hurricane hits land. Flooding from storm surges and heavy rain, like in 2005's Hurricane Katrina, causes more hurricane deaths than winds. Hurricanes are rated on the Saffir-Simpson scale of 1 to 5 (see page 15). The scale shows how these storms strengthen as their pressure drops.

Saffir-Simpson Scale

Category/Damage	Barometric pressure in inches (of mercury)	Wind speed in miles per hour (km/h)	Storm surge in feet
1-Minimal	more than 28.94	74–95 (119–153)	4–5
2-Moderate	28.50–28.91	96–110 (154–177)	6–8
3-Extensive	27.91–28.47	111–130 (178–209)	9–12
4-Extreme	27.17–27.88	131–155 (210–249)	13–18
5-Catastrophic	less than 27.17	more than 155 (249)	more than 18

Hurricane waves pummel a sea wall.

Hurricane Swirl

In this activity you can model the shape and pattern of a hurricane's winds and clouds—using water instead of air.

You'll Need

- water
- shallow cake pan
- cornstarch
- food coloring
- spoon
- paper and pencil (optional)

1. Fill the cake pan half full with water and stir a few spoonfuls of cornstarch into it until it looks milky.

2. When the water is more or less still, add one or two drops of food coloring into the center of the pan. Watch how the color sinks and moves.

3. Next, pull the spoon very slowly through the water. Watch for the trail of small spirals that form behind the spoon. You can draw the patterns, if you want.

4. "Erase" the color by thoroughly stirring the mixture and then letting the water settle again.

5. Add two or three more drops of food coloring in the center. This time use the handle of the spoon to make a circle around the drops. Compare it to the hurricane picture on page 13. You can draw the pattern, if you want.

Science Fair Spin

Does using warm or cold water change the swirling pattern? How about changing the size of the spoon? Design an experiment to find out.

Hurricane Hunter

Cool Weather Careers

Valerie Schmid is a meteorologist with a dangerous mission. She's a member of the United States Air Force Reserve's 53rd Weather Reconnaissance Squadron—the Hurricane Hunters. These pilots and scientists fly airplanes into the biggest storms on the planet to collect weather data needed to track hurricanes and issue life-saving alerts.

"Normally you're just so busy that you're not thinking this might be dangerous," says Schmid about working inside a plane that feels "like a bucking bronco" as it's being tossed in high winds and struck by lightning. She keeps her eye on the plane's weather instruments that record wind speeds, humidity, temperature, and air pressure.

Schmid first learned about the Hurricane Hunters from a movie she saw in high school. "I thought, 'Wow, what a cool job.' But I never thought I would be able to get a job like that," comments Schmid. But after studying meteorology in college and training in weather forecasting after joining the U.S. Air Force, she began thinking about flying through hurricanes. "I didn't like the math very much, but I stuck it out because I love science. Those two go hand in hand." And after becoming a qualified meteorologist in the air force she applied and was awarded a very competitive Hurricane Hunter position. "If you have a dream," says Schmid, "go for it!"

A Hurricane Hunter aircraft flies near the eye of Hurricane Caroline.

Ozone Layer Depletion

Weather and the Environment

About 12 to 30 miles (19 to 48 km) above the earth, near the top of the stratosphere, is the protective ozone layer. The layer is a band of ozone gas molecules, each made up of three oxygen atoms (O_3). The kind of oxygen gas you breathe has only two oxygen atoms (O_2). Ozone gas is created by the powerful sunlight at this altitude. Strong rays from the sun break up regular oxygen into single oxygen atoms. These lone oxygen atoms combine into triple-oxygen ozone, and then later break down again into regular oxygen (O_2). While oxygen is continually recombining like this, the ozone absorbs some of the sun's ultraviolet (UV) light. This UV absorption shields the earth from the full force of its harmful effects. Too much UV light can cause skin cancer and eye cataracts, and can damage plants and plankton.

In the late 1970s, scientists began to notice a thinning of the ozone layer over Antarctica during its frigid early spring. This soon-named "hole" in the ozone layer was carefully studied and researchers quickly realized that in fact ozone was thinning over both poles—arctic and Antarctic. The cause was chlorofluorocarbons (CFCs), super stable chlorine-containing chemicals. CFCs were used in air conditioners and refrigerators, as propellants in spray cans, in cleaning solvents for electronics, and to make disposable cups and other foam products. CFCs are so stable that once in the air they rise all the way to the stratosphere before they break down. When powerful sunlight in the stratosphere breaks up the CFCs, their chlorine destroys protective ozone. One CFC molecule can

Fast Fact

For several days during the winter of 1995–96, the ozone layer from Greenland to Siberia was depleted by 45 percent, according to the World Meteorological Organization.

destroy up to 100,000 molecules of ozone. The chlorine destroys so much ozone that the ozone layer thins, letting more dangerous UV light through to the earth.

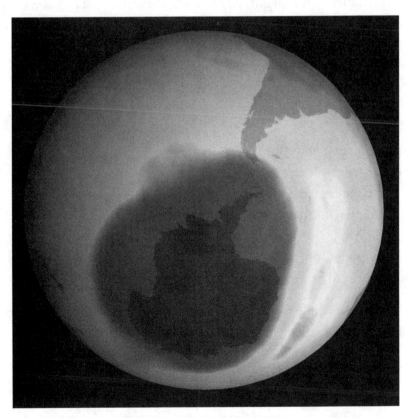

The largest ozone hole ever recorded was over the Antarctic in September 2000. It was 11 million square miles (28 million square kilometers). That's three times larger than the United States.

The United States, Canada, Norway, and Sweden banned the use of most CFC-based spray-can propellants in 1979. And the Montréal Protocol treaty of 1987 set in motion the phase-out of all CFC production. It has since been signed by 183 nations. Today the rate of ozone layer destruction is slowing. And scientists believe the ozone layer can repair itself given enough chlorine-free time. But it will likely take another 50 years for the ozone layer to return to normal.

- -

Screening out the Sun

The layer of upper atmospheric ozone gas screens out a good deal of harmful ultraviolet light, preventing it from reaching the earth's surface. In this activity, you can test the sun-blocking effects of a number of filters.

You'll Need
- ► 4 tuna, cat food, or other similarly sized cans with both ends removed
- ► 1 sheet of colored construction paper
- ► 3 different 4-inch square (10-cm square) filter covers (clear plastic wrap, colored plastic wrap, waxed paper, newspaper, cloth, aluminum foil, glass, etc.)
- ► tape
- ► pen, pencil, or marker
- ► sunny spot or windowsill

1. Assemble your filters. Tape a different filter cover onto the end of three of the cans. Leave one can uncovered.

2. Draw a line down the middle of the sheet of construction paper and one across the center so it's divided into four equal sections.

3. Put one filter on each of the paper's four sections. Label what each is, including the uncovered one.

4. Set the sheet of construction paper and filters in a sunny spot. (Use a stiff notebook or book as a tray to carry them.)

5. Leave the filters in the sun for a week. Then remove the filters and compare the paper underneath. Notice how much dye was bleached out by the sun through the different filter cover materials. Which blocked the most sunlight?

Science Fair Spin

Test the same filters, but on different colors of construction paper. Are some colors more easily bleached by the sun? Design an experiment to find out.

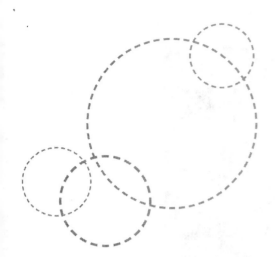

Sun and Seasons

We live on a solar-powered planet. Earth's weather is fueled by a medium-sized, middle-aged star of average brightness—the sun! The sun bathes our planet in light and heat. But the earth isn't evenly heated by the sun's energy. Differences in terrain, location on the globe, and the seasons result in an uneven heating of the earth's surfaces and in turn the atmosphere above them. On a given day the equator bakes while the poles freeze, for example. Likewise, a mountain town is much cooler than its valley neighbor. These global and local differences in temperature drive the weather engine on our planet. Earth's uneven heating leads to air masses of different temperatures, which cause pressure systems, fronts, and wind.

The sun gives Earth both light and heat.

Telling Time by the Sun

The sun's power to heat varies throughout the day as it travels across the sky. At noon, direct sunlight gives rise to warmer temperatures than at dawn, when sunlight is indirect and less concentrated, for example. Noting the sun's daily journey across the sky is also a way to tell time. An ancient instrument for tracking the sun, the sundial, was the most common timepiece until clocks and watches came into regular use in the 18th century. A sundial tells time using a marker, or **gnomon**, that casts a shadow on a sundial plate marked with numbers for the hours of the day. Make your own sundial and see for yourself!

You'll Need
- Sundial plate pattern on page 25
- cardboard
- glue
- large paper clip
- tape
- ruler

1. Trace or photocopy the sundial plate pattern on page 25. Then glue the pattern onto cardboard.

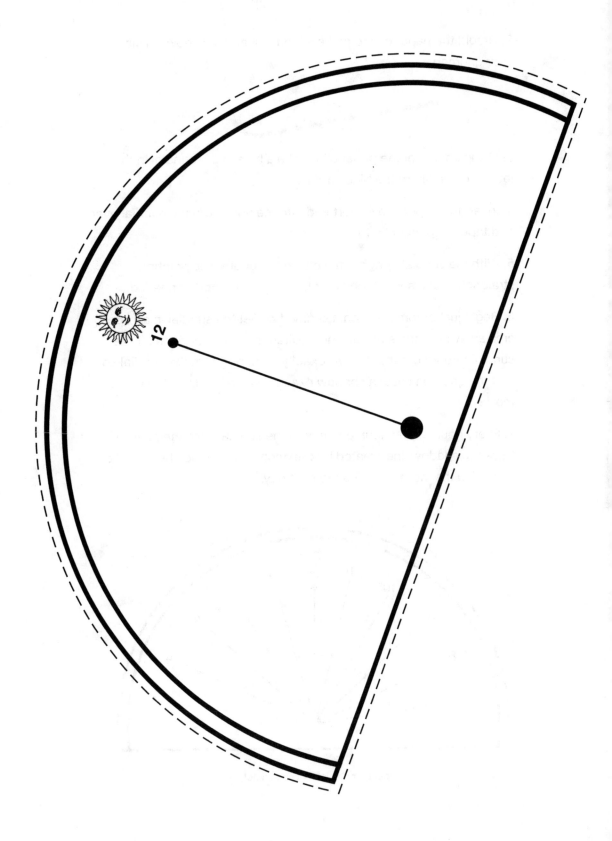

12

2. Unfold the paper clip to make a long L shape, as shown. This is your gnomon.

3. Using an end of the paper clip, poke a hole in the sundial in the lower center where the black dot is.

4. Insert the paper clip's short end into the hole. Turn the sundial over and tape the paper clip to the bottom.

5. With the sundial upright, make sure the gnomon is pointing straight up. Use some tape on both sides as support, if needed.

6. Begin just before noon on a sunny day. Set the sundial in an open area away from trees or buildings. (Direct sunlight needs to hit the sundial throughout the day.) At exactly 12 noon*, turn the sundial so that the gnomon casts a shadow exactly on the line from the dot to the 12.

7. Every hour, on the hour, go back to the sundial. Use the ruler to trace the shadow line created by the gnomon and label the hour. You can finish the morning hours the next day.

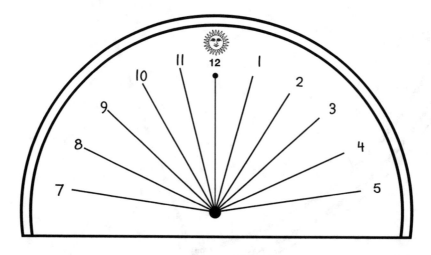

*Note: Sundials do not account for daylight savings time!

Science Fair Spin

*The sundial you created is only accurate for your specific north-south location, or **latitude**. Someone living farther north or south couldn't use your sundial to tell accurate time. Ask friends or relatives who live at different latitudes to create sundials using this activity and then send them to you for comparison. Can you design a model that replicates sunlight at the different latitudes using a gooseneck lamp?*

This giant sundial is on the island of St. Croix.

Sun Prints

Use the strength of sunlight to make art. Set a sheet of colored construction paper in a sunny spot, like a windowsill. Then arrange small heavy objects like coins, erasers, cups, etc., onto the colored paper. Leave your art project alone for a week or more. Then remove the objects and see the shapes left behind. The paper's dyes break down when exposed to sunlight.

 Fast Fact

The highest temperature ever recorded was 136°F (58°C) in Libya in September 1922. The lowest temperature was -128.6°F (-89.2°C) at Vostok Station in Antarctica during July 1983.

The Seasons

The earth rotates, or spins, on a tilted axis. That's why we have seasons. If the earth rotated in a perfectly upright position, all latitudes would have the same climate year 'round. But because of Earth's tilt, the northern and southern hemispheres receive different amounts of sunlight during the year. The northern hemisphere is tilted toward the sun during the summer, which means that the sun rises high in the sky, shining its light directly down on the surface and greatly heating it. In contrast, during winter the northern hemisphere is tilted away from the sun, so the sun is low in the sky. This means the sun's light reaches the surface at an indirect angle, causing the light to spread out over a greater area. The light is less concentrated during the winter so it heats less. In addition, because the sun's arc across the sky is so low during winter, it makes a much shorter path each day. This is why the day is shorter, which means even less warming sunlight.

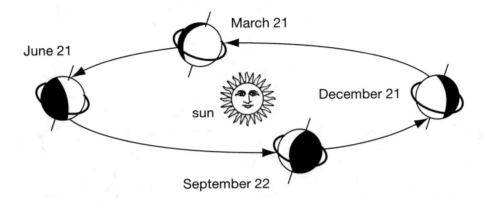

June 21

March 21

sun

December 21

September 22

Reason for Seasons

The earth's tilted axis causes different latitudes to receive varying amounts of sunlight throughout the year and creates our seasons. You can model how sunlight falls on different parts of the planet during the earth's rotation around the sun in this activity.

You'll Need
► globe
► lamp without a shade

1. Set the lamp on a desk or table in the center of a dimly lit or darkened room.

2. Find the northern and southern hemispheres, the poles, and equator on the globe. Also note how its axis is tilted.

3. Holding the globe, stand a few feet away from the lamp. Hold the globe away from your body somewhat so that the lamplight will hit it as you walk around the lamp. Keep your hands in the same position on the globe during the next steps.

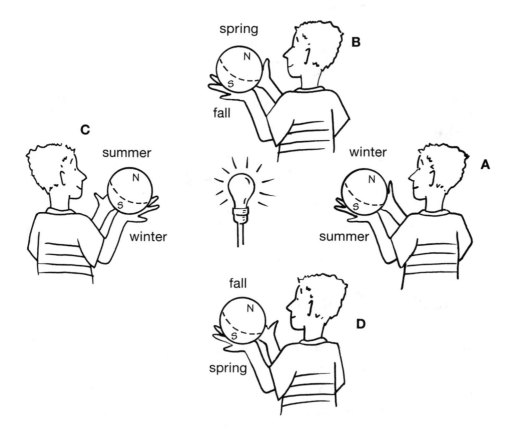

4. Start with the globe tilted, so that the southern hemisphere receives the most lamplight as in A above. This is summer in the southern hemisphere and winter in the northern hemisphere.

5. Move to position B above by walking to the right around the lamp. Now the equator is receiving the most light. This is spring in the northern hemisphere and fall in the southern hemisphere.

6. Move to position C above by continuing around the lamp, so that the northern hemisphere is receiving the most light. This is summer in the northern hemisphere and winter in the southern hemisphere.

7. Move to position D by continuing around the lamp. The equator is again receiving the most light. This is spring in the southern hemisphere and fall in the northern hemisphere.

Investigate and model the seasons on other planets in the solar system. The length and differences between a planet's seasons depend on that world's tilt and how fast it spins. On some planets, like Venus, seasons are shorter. But on others, seasons last longer. A single season can last for 20 years on Uranus.

Light Strength

You can see for yourself the difference that the angle of light makes. Simply shine a flashlight on a globe or ball. First hold the flashlight directly over the ball to model the strong direct light of summer. Note how it creates a perfect bright circle. Then shine the flashlight from the side, so that the light on the ball is more oval-shaped and less bright. This models the weaker indirect light of winter.

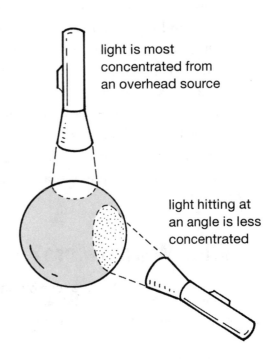

light is most concentrated from an overhead source

light hitting at an angle is less concentrated

Design an experiment that measures the temperature differences created by direct and indirect light.

Temperatures

Sunlight heats up land and water, which in turn heats the air above them. Temperature is the measure of how hot that air is. Scientifically, temperature is a measure of the speed that air molecules are moving. The faster that air molecules are moving, the higher their temperature.

The temperature on the earth's surface averages about 59°F (15°C) at sea level but ranges from about -130 to 140°F (-88 to 58°C) depending on the season, latitude, elevation, and time of day. The hottest time of day is usually mid-afternoon and the coldest is around dawn. The terrain greatly affects temperature because soil, water, and vegetation all absorb and give up heat at different rates. While land cools and warms quickly, water doesn't. So a lake's water can remain chilly even if its sandy beach is scorching hot. Dark areas absorb more heat than light areas, too. Areas covered in dark-colored rock absorb heat and warm up while a white snow-covered hill reflects sunlight and remains cool, for example. It's these differences in temperature at the earth's surface and up through the atmosphere that drive weather on our planet.

What Warms More?

How differently do water and land heat up and cool down? Find out for yourself in this activity.

You'll Need

- 3 identical containers that hold water (yogurt cups, soup cans, juice boxes, or milk cartons with the tops cut off, etc.)
- soil
- water
- 3 thermometers
- lamp
- watch or clock with second hand
- paper and pencil

Note: Set the soil, water, and thermometers in the room ahead of time so they'll be at equal temperatures for the activity.

1. Fill one container three-quarters full with water and another three-quarters full with soil. The last container remains "empty," though it's actually full of air.

2. Create a chart to record your results. You can photocopy the chart below or make your own. Your chart needs to have a place to record temperatures for all three containers at four different time intervals.

Temperature in °F / °C (circle one)

	0 minutes time _____	5 minutes time _____	10 minutes time _____	15 minutes time _____
soil				
water				
air				

3. Place a thermometer in each container. Make sure the thermometer bulb goes down into the soil. Write the time on your chart at 0 minutes and record a starting temperature for all three containers.

4. Go ahead and add five minutes to the starting time and write that time in the 5 minutes box. Do the same for the 10 and 15 minutes boxes, too, so you'll know when it's time to take temperatures.

5. Set the containers under a lamp, making sure that all three containers are equally exposed to the light. They can be close together, but shouldn't touch.

6. Read the temperatures at the correct time intervals and record them on the chart. Which heated up the most—air, soil, or water? The least?

Science Fair Spin

Design an experiment that compares the heating of different kinds of land—sand, rock, leaf-covered soil, etc. Or design an experiment that also compares which cools the fastest.

The Thermometer

A thermometer measures temperature. The great Italian scientist Galileo Galilee is usually credited with inventing the thermometer around 1592. It was likely a tube of glass filled with liquid and sealed at the bottom and open at the top. As the liquid heated, it expanded and rose up in the tube. More modern alcohol and mercury thermometers were invented by the German physicist Gabriel Fahrenheit in 1714. They worked on the same principle of a liquid expanding and rising in a tube. However, the tube was sealed on both ends. Fahrenheit also developed the standardized scale of temperature named after him in which water boils at 212°F and freezes at 32°F. The other common temperature scale, Celsius, or °C, was created only a few years later in 1742 by the Swedish astronomer Anders Celsius. The metric Celsius scale became more common worldwide than the Fahrenheit scale because it's simpler: water freezes at 0°C and boils at 100°C.

Fast Fact

Crickets are a fairly accurate thermometer. Just count the number of chirps in 14 seconds and add 40 to get degrees Fahrenheit.

Other kinds of thermometers and temperature scales have since been invented to serve the precision temperature-measuring needs of scientific research and industry. Electrical resistance thermometers use the resistivity of metals in relation to temperature to measure temperatures to .001°C in accuracy.

- -

Thermometer

Build a Weather Station

You can measure and track changes in temperature with this fun-to-make thermometer. It works on the same principle that a liquid thermometer does—the liquid (water) expands as it heats up. Note that the units on the scale are only relative and will not be accurate at or below the freezing point because water expands when frozen.

You'll Need

- ▶ 16 oz. (473 ml) glass bottle
- ▶ 2 white or clear straws
- ▶ water
- ▶ food coloring
- ▶ modeling clay
- ▶ glue
- ▶ index card
- ▶ vegetable or mineral oil (optional)

1. Roll the clay into a ball. Its diameter needs to be slightly larger than the mouth of the bottle.

2. Set the clay ball on a table. Use one of the straws to poke a hole through the center of the ball of clay. Try to make the hole as straight and as clean as you can. Once the hole goes completely through the clay ball, pull the straw out. (Mess it up? Just start over!)

3. Carefully push a new straw into the hole made in step 2. Push it until the straw is about one-third of the way though. Pinch and pat the clay around the straw on both sides to make a tight seal.

4. Fill the bottle with water. It needs to be filled to the top. Add a few drops of food coloring so the water will be easier to see as it travels up the straw.

5. Place the straw with the ball of clay into the bottle—long straw end first. Firmly press down on the ball of clay at the bottle's mouth to make an airtight seal. Colored water should rise up into the straw beyond the mouth of the bottle. If it doesn't, just pour a little extra colored water into the straw. (Note: If the water doesn't stay in the straw, there's leakage around the bottle's mouth, so you'll need to reseal it.) If you'll be using the thermometer for a few days, add a drop of clear baby oil into the top of the straw to prevent evaporation.

6. Trace or photocopy the thermometer scale below, or create your own. Glue the scale onto an index card and cut it out. Carefully slide the scale into the clay just behind the straw. A little glue will help keep it there.

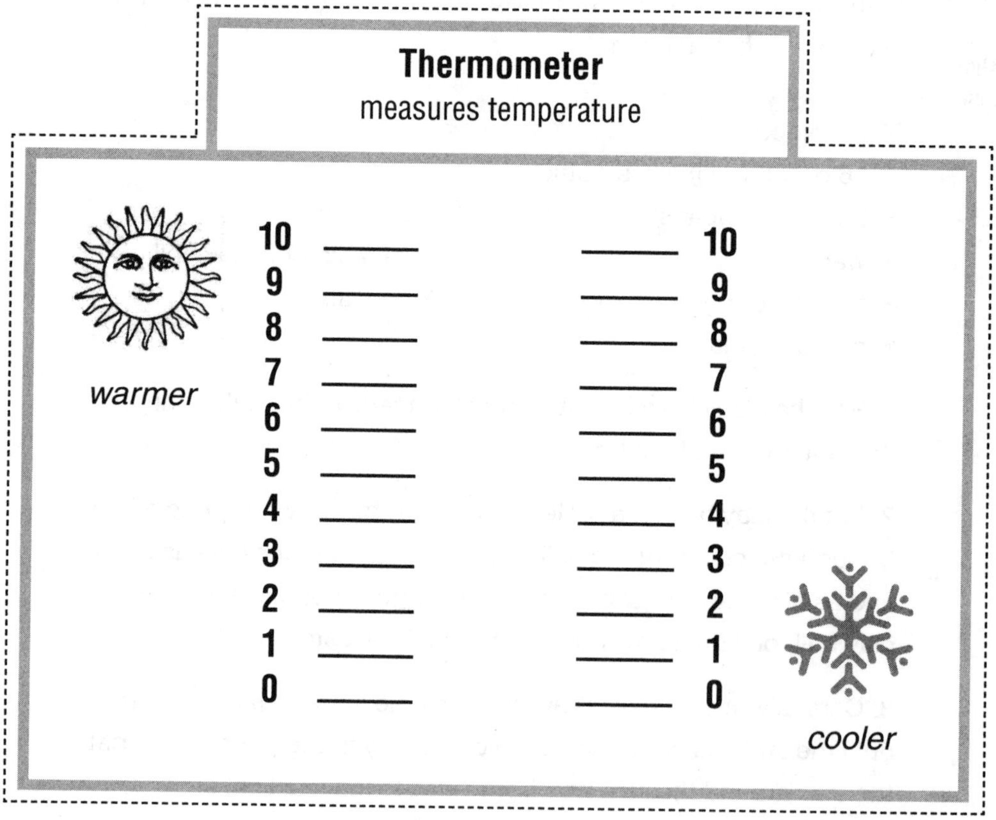

Thermometer

measures temperature

warmer

10 —
9 —
8 —
7 —
6 —
5 —
4 —
3 —
2 —
1 —
0 —

— 10
— 9
— 8
— 7
— 6
— 5
— 4
— 3
— 2
— 1
— 0

cooler

Thermometer
measures temperature

warmer

cooler

7. You can test out your thermometer in some "extreme" conditions such as in the refrigerator or near a heat vent or sunny window. The water level will rise and fall as it contracts and expands in response to changes in temperature. You can also track temperatures over time. Creating a chart with the following headings can help: DATE, TIME, READING, THERMOMETER LOCATION.

Science Fair Spin

What other liquids besides water might expand with rising temperatures and work in a thermometer? Design an experiment that uses different liquids in the above thermometer and test them for accuracy.

Air Masses

Sunlight heats the land and water, which in turn heats the air above them. When air stays over an area of land or water for many days it tends to stabilize to an even temperature and humidity based on how cold, warm, dry, or wet the land below it is. The air becomes an air mass, a chunk of atmosphere that has a uniform temperature and humidity.

Air masses are huge, often the size of a couple of states. Most warm air masses form in the tropics and most cold ones at high latitudes. (It's difficult for air masses to form in the middle latitudes where air doesn't stay in one place very long.) Cold air masses move away from the poles toward warmer areas and warm air masses move away from the tropics toward cooler areas. This is how the earth balances its heat budget to keep the poles from getting continually colder and the tropics from getting continually warmer. (Global ocean currents also help balance Earth's heat budget.) Whether or not the air masses are wet or dry depends on where they formed—over water or land.

Fronts

Air masses all over the globe are on the move—and they often meet. But air masses don't easily mix. Cold air is heavier than warm air, so air masses with different temperatures remain separate like oil and water. The boundary where two different air masses collide is called a front. It's a battleground of weather, where one air mass advances while another retreats—creating storms and weather changes as a result. If warm air is advancing, it's called a **warm front**. If cold air is pushing on the boundary, it's a **cold front**. If it's a standoff, it's a **stationary front**.

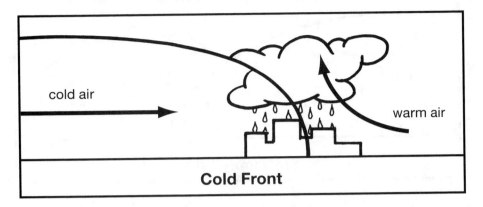

Cold Front

In a cold front, heavier cold air wedges under lighter warm air, shoving it upward. The dividing line between the air masses in a cold front is a steeper slope than in a warm front. The cold air shoves against the warm air like a snowplow. This often causes sudden and violent changes in weather. Cold fronts usually bring brief heavy **precipitation** and then colder temperatures.

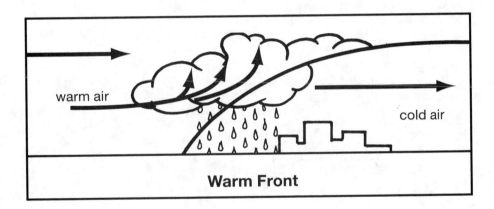

Warm Front

In a warm front, lighter warm air slides up and over the heavier, denser cold air. The boundary has a long gentle slope from the ground up into the atmosphere. Warm fronts generally bring steady precipitation for a long time over a large area and warmer temperatures.

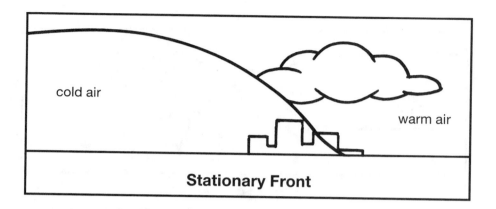

In a stationary front neither air mass is gaining. Clouds can form along the sides of the boundary, but precipitation is usually off and on—if at all—and is unlikely to include thunderstorms.

A cold front moves in over Lake Erie.

Full of Hot Air

Air masses and the fronts their collisions create generate much of our weather. Discover for yourself the weather-creating power of rising hot air in this activity.

You'll Need

- ▶ small bottle with narrow opening
- ▶ small balloon
- ▶ cold water
- ▶ hot water
- ▶ ice
- ▶ 2 flat-bottomed dishes or containers
- ▶ marbles, pennies, pebbles (anything to add weight to the bottle)

1. Fill one dish about halfway with cold tap water. Put a few ice cubes in it.

2. Put an inch or so of weights (marbles, pennies, etc.) in the bottle. Make sure the bottle doesn't float by setting it in the dish of water. If it does float, add more weights.

3. Cap the bottle with a small balloon. Be careful not to tear a hole in the balloon.

4. Fill the other dish halfway with hot tap water. First set the balloon-topped bottle into the dish of hot water. Why does the balloon inflate?

5. Once the balloon has popped up, move it to the dish of cold water. What happens? What causes the balloon to shrink?

Monsoons

The monsoons are a seasonal wind that brings rain by carrying moist ocean air in toward land. The word **monsoon** comes from

Storm Science

the Arabic word for season, *mausim*. Monsoon rains fall in many areas of the tropics and subtropics including parts of northeast Australia, East Africa, the Caribbean, South America, and the southeastern United States. But the Asian monsoons are the most extreme— and famous.

From October to April most of India is dry and dusty. Dry winter air over the cooling land is heavy, so it sinks down on Asia. This creates a large high-pressure area over the continent. Air moves from the high pressure over the continent to lower pressure over the Indian Ocean, creating dry winter winds

> ### 🐦 Fast Fact
>
> The Indian town of Cherrapunji averages 425 inches (1,080 cm) of rain a year and once received 1,042 inches (2,647 cm) during a 12-month period.

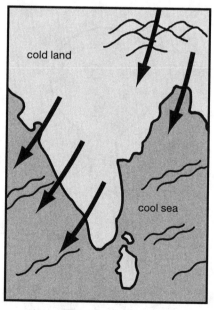

Dry Northeast Monsoon (October–April).

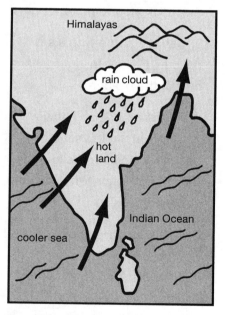

Wet Southwest Monsoon (May–September).

blowing off the continent toward the water. But because of the seasonal tilt of the earth, come late April or May the land begins to heat up from more direct sunlight. The air above the land heats up much faster than the air above the slower-warming ocean. Atmospheric pressure over the continent falls as it warms, and air moves in from the cooler and higher-pressure ocean to replace the rising air mass over the warm land. The wind directions have switched, and they now bring moisture-soaked air off the ocean that rains out in drenching storms as the air moves up toward Asia's Himalayan mountains.

The monsoons bring a lot of rain. The world's highest rainfall averages are in monsoon areas, and the rains brought by monsoons are the only rains some regions get all year. Nearly half of the world's population depends on monsoon rains to grow crops.

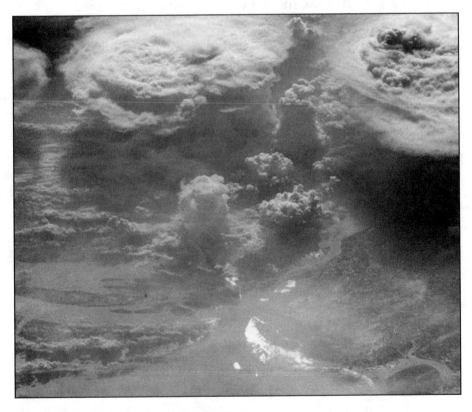

Monsoon clouds building over Bangladesh.

Global Climate Change

When the earth's surface is warmed by the sun, gases in the atmosphere soak up and radiate back much of that heat. The gases act like a blanket that traps body heat. Take away the atmosphere (like on the moon) and the average temperature on Earth would fall from its current 60°F to about 0°F. An atmosphere's warming ability is often called the **greenhouse effect**. (This isn't a great name! The air inside a greenhouse stays warm because the glass traps in sun-warmed air, unlike an atmosphere that radiates back heat.)

Weather and the Environment

The "greenhouse gases" that absorb and radiate heat back to Earth make our planet habitable. Water vapor is the most common greenhouse gas, which is why cloudy nights are warmer than clear ones. The clouds hold the heat in. Other greenhouse gases include carbon dioxide, methane, nitrous oxide, and chlorofluorocarbons (CFCs). Though some greenhouse gases occur naturally, their concentrations have increased over the past hundred years as humans burn fossil fuels and pollute. Cutting down forests has also added carbon dioxide to the atmosphere because trees—like all green plants—absorb carbon dioxide to produce food.

With more greenhouse gases in the atmosphere, the earth is now additionally warmed by the denser blanket of gases. This is called global warming, but a more accurate name for this is global climate change because as the earth's overall temperature increases, some areas may warm while others may actually cool. It's estimated that Earth's average temperature has risen about 1.8 °F (1 °C) since 1850. A United Nations panel of scientists predicts an expected rise of another 6°F (3.3°C) in the next century if greenhouse-gas emissions aren't reduced.

A few degrees warmer may not seem like much to worry about, but a rise of 3.6°F (2°C) means sea level will likely rise 20 inches (51 cm) from melting ice caps and the expansion of water as it warms. Many coastal cities would flood if not be completely destroyed, and some low-lying islands could eventually disappear.

Temperature changes will also likely change many global weather patterns as winds and currents are altered, disrupting ecosystems and agriculture.

The global climate is a very complicated system that scientists still have many unanswered questions about. But most scientists believe human activity is changing the current climate. The United Nations called for a climate summit in December 1997 that was held in Kyoto, Japan. It resulted in the Kyoto Protocol, a historic environmental agreement that calls for industrialized countries to fight global warming by cutting back on the amount of harmful carbon dioxide and other greenhouse-gas emissions from 2008 through 2012. A total of 153 countries have agreed to the Kyoto Protocol. But some nations, including the United States and Australia, have refused to participate in the treaty.

This National Oceanic and Atmospheric Administration station at the South Pole samples the atmosphere for greenhouse gases.

Hothouse Heat Up

In this activity, you can discover how trapping heat increases temperatures. (Note: The plastic wrap represents the heat-trapping greenhouse gases in the atmosphere, but is not a perfect model for how the atmosphere traps heat since gases absorb and radiate heat back.)

You'll Need

- 2 identical tall containers (quart tubs, tall cans, milk or juice cartons with the tops cut off, etc.)
- dark potting soil
- plastic wrap
- 2 thermometers
- lamp
- watch or clock with second hand
- two pens or pencils of different colors

1. Fill both containers half full of soil. Set the thermometers into the soil, but not so deep that you can't read them. Make sure both are identically placed.

2. Tightly cover the top of one soil-filled container with plastic wrap. If the wrap isn't snug, use rubber bands or tape to secure it.

3. Photocopy the graph on page 47, or create your own using graph paper. This is where you'll record the temperatures. Choose pens to record the covered and uncovered soil-sample temperatures. Make a key with the pens' colors on the graph.

4. Set the containers under a lamp so that both are equally exposed to the light. They can be close together, but shouldn't touch.

5. Write a start time on the graph, note each temperature, and plot both points on the graph. Add 5 minutes to the starting time and write that time under the 5-minute line and do the same for all time intervals. (The end time should be 30 minutes later than the start time.)

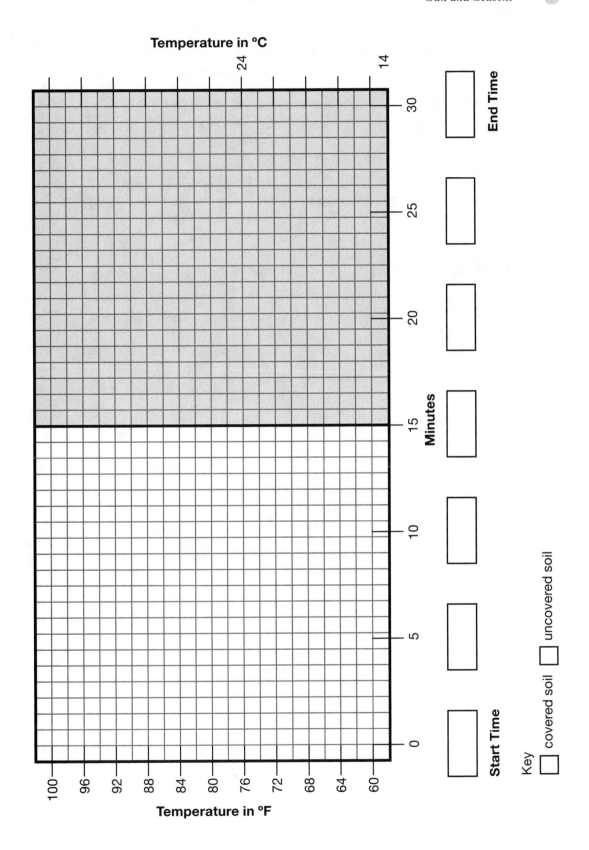

Temperature in °C

Temperature in °F

Minutes

Start Time   End Time

Key

covered soil   uncovered soil

6. Take the temperature of the containers at 5, 10, and 15 minutes from the start time and plot the points on the graph.

7. After taking the 15-minute temperatures, TURN OFF THE LAMP. Then continue to read and plot the temperatures at 20, 25, and 30 minutes.

8. Once all the temperatures have been plotted, compare the two graph lines. Which heated up the fastest? Cooled the fastest? Why?

Design an experiment that compares the heating and cooling rates of the samples using different kinds of lamp light (incandescent, florescent, halogen, etc.).

Science Fair Spin

Systems Scientist

Cool Weather Careers

Brian O'Neill's job is predicting the future. The future of the earth's climate, that is. Scientists estimate that our planet's temperature has risen about 1.8°F (1°C) due to global climate change (see Weather and the Environment: Global Climate Change on page 44).

The temperature will likely continue to rise as our growing world emits increasing amounts of greenhouse gases. But exactly what a warmer Earth will be like is unknown. What will the growing season be like in Russia? How much will the sea level rise by 2050? And how much difference would cleaner cars or factories make? "What if the United States reduces greenhouse-gas emissions?" asks O'Neill. "How much better off would the climate be?"

These are questions that scientists like O'Neill are trying to answer. He's an Earth Systems scientist at Brown University. The means of predicting the future for scientists like O'Neill is the computer. Information collected about Earth's past climate as well as current conditions is processed by powerful data-crunching computers to model what might happen in the future. Computer modeling like this can predict what the climatic conditions on Earth would be like if emissions were reduced and allows scientists to pinpoint how best to deal with the problem. "It allows us to look at the implications of environmental policies like the Kyoto Protocol," explains O'Neill. It also allows them to plan for the future.

But predicting the future isn't easy. The earth's climate is complicated business. The amount of carbon dioxide in the air is influenced by ocean currents, forest size, ocean chemistry, and atmospheric conditions as well as how much pollution people make. But that's what keeps O'Neill fascinated. "Global climate change is connected to the whole history of the planet. This is the same system that's kept life around for billions of years and taken us in and out of ice ages," he says.

Arctic and Antarctic wildlife are especially vulnerable to global warming. Too much ice melting affects their yearly migrations, breeding sites, and food sources.

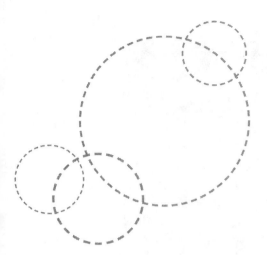

Clouds and Rain

The Water Cycle

Our world is a watery place. Oceans cover more than 70 percent of the surface of the earth. Added to that is the water in rivers, lakes, streams, ponds, and polar ice. Even the air around us—the atmosphere—contains an enormous amount of water in the form of water vapor, a gas. The constant movement of water back and forth between the earth's surface and the atmosphere is called the water cycle. The water cycle is powered by heat and water's ability to easily change phase, or switch between a liquid, gas, and solid.

Heated liquid water changes into water vapor during evaporation (the transition of a liquid to a gas). As water vapor rises, it cools, and the molecules of water form droplets. This is called con-

Water that's evaporated from the earth's surface condenses into clouds that produce rain that in turn falls back to Earth.

densation (the transition of a gas to a liquid) or sublimation (the transition of a gas to a solid) if it's cold enough for the water vapor to form ice crystals. Water vapor condensing into tiny droplets around dust, smoke, or other condensation nuclei creates clouds. If the droplets grow too large and heavy to be held up by air currents, they fall to the ground as precipitation—rain, sleet, snow, etc.

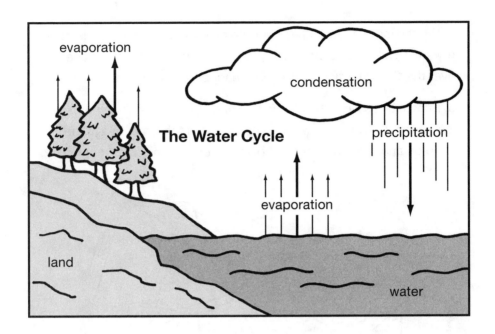

Cycling Water

The water cycle explains how clouds form and why rain falls. Create and observe a mini-water cycle that goes through evaporation, condensation, and precipitation in this activity.

You'll Need
▶ clear plastic carryout or produce box, or
   glass loaf pan with a clear lid
▶ small bowl
▶ warm water
▶ ice cubes
▶ zipper-closing plastic bag
▶ strong lamp

1. Set the bowl inside the box at one end. Fill the bowl halfway with warm tap water. This is your "lake." Close the lid.

2. Put the lamp a few inches over the box's lid directly over the bowl of water. The lamp is the "sun." Turn the "sun" on and let it shine over the "lake" for two hours. What happens to the water?

3. Put ice cubes into the plastic bag and zip it closed. Set the bag of ice on top of the lid at the opposite end from the lamp. Leave the lamp on and wait another two hours. Where did the "rain" come from?

Changing State

Changing water vapor to a liquid or solid or changing liquid water to ice requires cooling. When water cools, heat moves out of the water and into the surrounding air. On the other hand, changing ice to liquid water or liquid water to water vapor requires added heat. The heat needed to melt ice or evaporate water moves in from surrounding air, so the surrounding air in turn is cooled. (This is how sweating cools you. As the water evaporates on your skin, it pulls heat out of your body.) The heat that water adds and subtracts from surrounding air when it changes phase is called latent heat. Latent heat fuels many kinds of storms.

Powerful Changes

Discover the power of latent heat for yourself by measuring how much heat is released and absorbed during a phase change.

You'll Need
- ▶ 2 thermometers
- ▶ strip of absorbent cloth or paper towel
- ▶ water
- ▶ paper and pencil
- ▶ freezer
- ▶ ice cube tray
- ▶ rubber band (optional)

1. Wrap the bulb of a thermometer in the strip of cloth. You can use a rubber band to attach it if the cloth won't stay on.

2. Read the temperature and write it down.

3. Wet the cloth-wrapped thermometer bulb with water. Wave it in the air to help the water evaporate for a minute or two.

4. Read the temperature. How many degrees of heat were lost during evaporation? Where did that heat go?

5. Unwrap the thermometer and let it come to room temperature. Meanwhile, fill an ice cube tray with cold water and set it inside a freezer.

6. Place one of the thermometers inside the freezer on top of the ice cube tray. Make sure its bulb isn't sticking down into the water in the tray. You want to take the temperature of the air above the water, not of the water itself.

7. Set the other thermometer inside the freezer away from the ice cube tray.

8. Read the thermometers and write down their temperatures every 10 minutes until the ice cubes form.

9. How many degrees of heat were gained by the air above the ice cubes as they changed into solid water? Where did that heat come from?

Precipitation

Rain, sleet, hail, snow, or any other form of water that falls out of clouds is called precipitation. The particular kind of precipitation it is depends on its size, the temperature of the cloud it came from, and the temperature of the air it fell through. Drizzle, for example, is made up of liquid water drops less than 0.02 inches (0.5 mm) in diameter. Rain is liquid precipitation larger than 0.02 inches (0.5 mm). Freezing rain falls to the ground as liquid water and then freezes into ice on contact with any surface. Sleet is made of raindrops that have frozen in mid-air. Snow, on the other hand, is made up of ice crystals. (See Winter Storms on page 121.) Hailstones are balls of ice that usually form from clusters of raindrops frozen in thunderstorm updrafts. Fog isn't precipitation at all. It's simply a cloud at ground level.

> **Fast Fact**
>
> On an average day 40,000 billion gallons (151,400 billion liters) of water—as water vapor and clouds—are in the atmosphere over the United States alone.

Freezing rain falls as liquid water and then freezes into an icy layer covering sidewalks, streets, and tree branches.

Rain Gauge

This easy-to-make rain gauge will allow you to measure rainfall in your area.

You'll Need

► 1- or 2-liter plastic bottle

► weights (marbles, aquarium gravel, stones, pennies, etc.)

► scissors

► clear packing tape

► water

► ruler (optional)

1. Carefully cut the plastic bottle where the sides start to slope up to the mouth. Put tape around both cut edges. The top will act as a funnel.

2. Place enough weights into the bottom of the large half of the bottle to stabilize it.

3. Set the funnel inside the bottle so the taped edges touch.

4. Trace or photocopy the rain gauge scale on page 58, or create your own using a ruler. Cut out the scale and tape it onto the outside of the bottle. Make sure the "0" line is above the weights and at a level where the bottle's shape is uniform. Use clear packing tape to completely cover the scale so it's waterproof.

5. Pour water into the gauge until it reaches the "0" line on the bottom

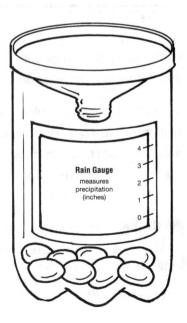

Rain Gauge

measures
precipitation
(inches)

4
3
2
1
0

Rain Gauge
measures
precipitation
(inches)

4

3

2

1

0

4

3

2

1

0

of the scale. The gauge will need to be reset to this "0" level each day that rainfall is to be measured.

6. Set the rain gauge outside in an open area, avoiding trees and building overhangs. Record (and then reset) the rain gauge at the same time each day to measure daily rainfall. Creating a chart with the following headings can help: DATE, TIME, INCHES OF RAIN.

Science Fair Spin

Is it winter now? Design an instrument to measure snow instead of rain. Here's a hint: it takes 10 inches of snow to equal the amount of liquid water in 1 inch of rain.

Homemade Rainbow

Nothing's nicer after a hard downpour than seeing a beautiful rainbow. Rainbows are often seen after storms because rain is still falling in another part of the sky while the sun is to the viewer's back—a rainbow's recipe. A rainbow's colors come from white sunlight being split into a spectrum of colors by raindrops acting like tiny prisms. A rainbow's arch shape is part of a circle made by the roundness of raindrops. You'll use water to break up light into the colors of a rainbow in this activity.

You'll Need
► small mirror
► clear bowl or container
► 8-by-11-inch (20-by-28-cm) piece of white poster board
► water
► sunny window

1. Fill the bowl or container with water and set it in direct sunlight. Place the mirror in the water facing the sunlight. Set the poster board between the container and the window.

2. Adjust the angle of the mirror until it casts a rainbow on the poster board. Enjoy!

Sleet vs. Snow

Snow and sleet are both frozen precipitation, but they fall very differently from the sky because of their differences in weight and shape. Snowflakes are large crystals of ice that float down slowly because their large flat shape creates air resistance, like a parachute. Sleet is bits of heavy solid ice that speed toward the ground like tiny rocks. In this activity you can discover how weight and shape affect the speed of falling.

You'll Need
- uncooked rice
- corn flakes
- chair
- newspaper
- friend

1. Spread newspaper on the floor and set a chair on it. (You can also do this outside, if it's not windy.)

2. Mix ½ cup (118 ml) rice and ½ cup (118 ml) corn flakes in the cupped hands of your friend.

3. Ask the friend to stand on the chair, carefully holding the cupped cereal and rice. You need to stand back five or so feet from the chair.

4. Have your friend raise her or his hands up high and then let the rice and cereal fall while you watch. Which hit the ground first—the snow-like corn flakes or sleet-like rice? Why?

Make Snow Globes

Everybody loves those fun snow globe souvenirs that you shake to make a memorable scene snow again and again. Here's how to make your own personal "shake and snow" snow globe.

You'll Need
- ▶ baby food or other small jar with lid
- ▶ plasticine clay
- ▶ small plastic objects (optional)
- ▶ waterproof glue
- ▶ white and/or silver glitter

1. Create a scene on the upturned jar lid using plasticine clay, plastic objects, or whatever else you'd like. Remember that the scene will have to fit inside the jar. Also make sure everything is waterproof and well glued down with waterproof glue. Let the scene completely dry.

2. Fill the jar about three-quarters full with water and add a pinch of silver and/or white glitter. Carefully top the jar with the scene-covered lid and tightly screw it closed. (If it isn't watertight, seal with glue.)

3. Gently shake the jar to make your scene snowy!

Rain Prints

A fun rainy-day activity is to make rain prints.

You'll Need
- rainy day
- rubber band
- old pantyhose, tights, or other thin, stretchy material
- empty coffee can
- flour sifter
- powdered sugar

1. Use a rubber band to secure a piece of old pantyhose over an empty coffee can.

2. Use a flour sifter to sprinkle a fine layer of powered sugar over the pantyhose.

3. Set the can outside in the rain for a few seconds. Once back inside observe and compare the raindrop prints made in the sugar. Are they all the same size and shape? Are they evenly spaced?

Humidity and Dew Point

Humidity is the amount of water vapor in the air. All air holds some water vapor, even dry desert air. The amount of water vapor that air can hold depends on the air's temperature. Cold air can hold less water vapor than warm air before that water vapor condenses into liquid water. The faster-moving molecules in warm air mean that more water can remain as vapor without being condensed into liquid. Air's ability to hold water vapor roughly doubles with each 50°F (10°C) in temperature increase. The temperature at which air loses its ability to hold water vapor and condensation occurs is called the dew point. It's the temperature of the air when dew—water vapor condensing to liquid—forms. If the dew point temperature is below freezing, frost forms instead.

 Fast Fact

The same moisture-carrying 86°F (30°C) and 42 percent relative-humidity air will change to 100 percent relative humidity if the temperature drops to 59°F (15°C).

The amount of water vapor in the air is referred to in two different ways. Meteorologists want to know the specific humidity, or the actual amount of water in the air. Specific humidity is usually measured in parts per thousand. Weather reporters, however, usually talk about the relative humidity. Relative humidity is the specific humidity divided by the vapor-holding capacity of air at a given temperature. A relative humidity reading of 75 percent means that the air contains 75 percent of the water vapor it can possibly hold for that particular temperature. Although the specific humidity might not change all day, the relative humidity will change as the temperature rises and falls.

Do the Dew Point

Glasses filled with cold drinks "sweat" because they cool the air immediately around them to the dew point—the temperature at which water vapor in the air condenses to liquids. You can use this fact to find the dew-point temperature where you are in this activity.

You'll Need

► metal can with label and top removed
► ice
► room-temperature water
► thermometer
► paper and pencil

1. Fill the can about halfway with room-temperature water. Make sure the outside of the can is dry.

2. Place the thermometer in the can and record the temperature. Leave the thermometer in the can.

3. Add a few ice cubes and stir. Carefully watch the outside of the can for "sweat" droplets of dew to form. When they do, record the temperature. This is the dew-point temperature.

Science Fair Spin

Use this setup to compare dew points under different conditions of humidity and temperature— outside, basement, attic, steamy bathroom, etc.

Make Frost

Frost is water vapor that sublimated (changed from a gas to a solid) instead of condensing into dew. You can sublimate some frost for yourself in this activity.

You'll Need

► metal can with label and top removed

► ice

► rock salt

► spoon

► magnifying lens

► paper and pencil (optional)

1. Fill the can with ice and rock salt. Make sure the outside of the can is dry.

2. Start stirring the ice and salt with a spoon.

3. Carefully watch the outside of the can. After stirring for a while frost will form as the room's water vapor freezes onto the can.

4. Once frost has formed, observe it with the magnifying lens. You can sketch the crystal patterns of the frost, too.

Design an experiment that compares how long it takes for frost to form depending on the room's temperature.

Science Fair Spin

The Hygrometer and Psychrometer

A hygrometer is any instrument that measures atmospheric humidity, or the amount of water vapor in the air. Many hygrometers simply indicate whether or not the air contains significant moisture. Hygrometers using human hairs have been created for this purpose for many centuries. When a hair—or other fiber—is wet, it lengthens. Hair hygrometers come in many shapes, including whimsical weather houses where different residents pop in and out depending on the humidity.

The psychrometer is a type of hygrometer used to measure relative humidity. It's often called a wet-and-dry bulb thermometer because it's made of two thermometers, one with a normal dry bulb and another with a bulb wrapped in wet cloth. The wet bulb thermometer is cooled by evaporation, the amount of which is dependent on the amount of water vapor in the air. (The drier the air, the faster the water will evaporate and the more the wet bulb will cool.) The difference between the dry and wet thermometer's readings is used to calculate relative humidity on a table of temperatures.

Psychrometer

You can accurately measure relative humidity with this wet-and-dry bulb thermometer, or psychrometer.

Build a Weather Station

You'll Need
▶ half-gallon plastic milk or juice jug with lid
▶ scissors
▶ 2 Fahrenheit thermometers
▶ cotton shoestring with tips cut off or a 6-by-1-inch (15-by-3-cm) strip of absorbent cloth
▶ rubber bands
▶ permanent marker or grease pencil

1. Ask an adult to help you carefully cut a dime-sized hole about 2 inches (5 cm) from the bottom of the jug on one of the sides.

2. Wrap the bulb of one of the thermometers with one end of the shoestring and use a rubber band to secure it. It needs to have a 3-inch (7.5-cm) "tail" remaining.

3. Thread the shoestring tail through the hole and use a rubber band to attach the thermometer to the outside of the carton. Write WET-BULB above or below it.

4. Use another rubber band to attach the other thermometer to an adjacent side of the jug. Write DRY-BULB above or below it.

5. Pour water into the jug until the shoelace soaks up water, but doesn't leak out the hole. Let the water and thermometers come to room

temperature and make sure the shoelace is soaking up water. The shoestring around the bulb should feel wet.

6. Air needs to move past the wet-bulb to ensure an accurate reading. You can fan the air around the wet-bulb thermometer using a folder or piece of cardboard.

7. Record both the wet and dry bulb temperatures and use the table below to determine relative humidity.

8. You can record and track the daily humidity on a chart by repeating steps 6 and 7. Creating a chart with the following headings can help: DATE, TIME, WET-BULB TEMP, DRY-BULB TEMP, RELATIVE HUMIDITY, WEATHER (Sunny, Cloudy, Rainy?)

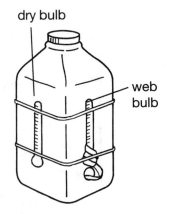
dry bulb
web bulb

dry-bulb temperatures (°F)

wet-bulb temp (°F)	56	58	60	62	64	66	68	70	71	72	73	74	75	76	77	78	79	80	82	84	86	88
38	7	2																				
40	15	11	7																			
42	25	19	14	9	7																	
44	34	29	22	17	13	8	4															
46	45	38	30	24	18	14	10	6	4	3	1											
48	55	47	40	33	26	21	16	12	10	9	7	5	4	3	1							
50	66	56	48	41	34	29	23	19	17	15	13	11	9	8	6	5	4	3				
52	77	67	57	50	43	36	31	25	23	21	19	17	15	13	12	10	9	7	5	3	1	
54	88	76	68	59	51	44	38	33	30	28	25	23	21	19	17	16	14	12	10	7	5	3
56		89	79	66	60	53	46	40	37	34	32	29	27	25	23	21	19	18	14	12	9	7
58			89	79	70	61	54	48	45	42	39	36	34	31	29	27	25	23	20	18	14	11
60				90	79	71	62	55	52	48	46	43	40	38	35	33	31	29	25	21	18	15
62					90	80	71	64	60	57	53	50	47	44	42	39	37	35	30	28	23	20
64						90	80	72	68	65	61	58	54	51	48	46	43	41	36	32	28	25
66							90	81	77	73	69	65	62	59	58	53	50	47	42	37	33	30
68								90	86	82	78	74	70	66	63	60	57	54	48	43	39	35
70									95	91	88	82	78	74	71	67	64	61	55	49	44	40
72											95	91	88	82	79	75	71	68	61	56	50	46
74													96	91	87	83	79	75	69	62	57	51
76															96	91	87	83	76	69	63	57
78																	96	91	84	78	70	64
80																			82	84	77	70
82																				92	84	77
84																					92	85
86																						92

Cloud Types

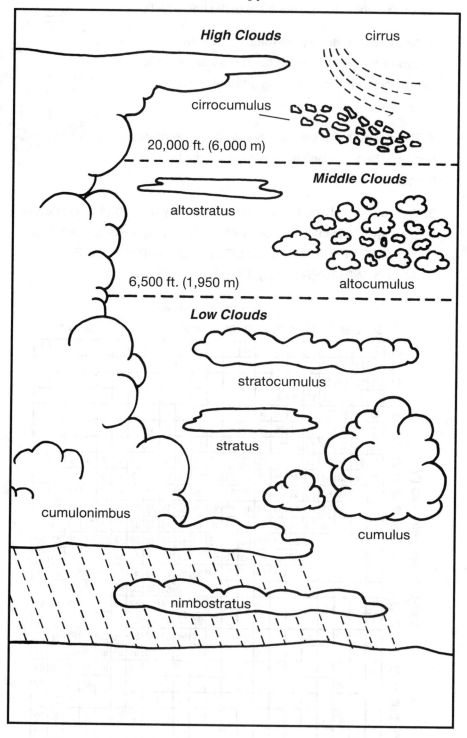

Clouds

Clouds are made of tiny water droplets and/or ice crystals suspended by air and updrafts. Air is able to hold up the water droplets in clouds because they're so small. It takes a million cloud drops to make a single rain drop. When cloud droplets or ice crystals grow large, they fall as precipitation.

Clouds are classified into many different identifiable types. The names of clouds are made up of Latin words that describe their general shape and often the height where they're found. Most cloud names are one of three cloud shapes—cirrus, **stratus**, and **cumulus**. Cirrus are curly- or stringy-looking clouds made of ice crystals.

High, wispy cirrus clouds on a bright winter day.

Stratus clouds are stratified or layered and flat. Cumulus are lumpy, fluffy, often piled-up clouds. The shape name can be combined with a prefix like cirro-, alto-, and nimbo-. Cirro- means the cloud is high, a base above 20,000 feet (6 km) or so. Alto- means mid-level, or about 6,000-20,000 feet (2–6 km). There is no prefix for low. The prefix or suffix -nimbo- means the cloud is making precipitation. Therefore, a cirrocumulus is a high, fluffy cloud while a cumulonimbus is a piled-up, rain-making cloud. Stratocumulus is an exception, the name being made up of two shapes, but they do look both lumpy and stratified.

Frame a Cloud

A fun way to become familiar with cloud shapes and start learning to identify them is to capture one in a "frame." Use masking tape to frame a cloud seen through a window. Then draw the cloud a number of times over a few minutes as the cloud moves out of the frame. Use the Cloud Types diagram on page 68 to try to identify your captured cloud.

Clouds and Weather

Clouds look different because they are formed by different kinds of winds and mixes of ice and water. Cirrus clouds are so high, for example, that they are made of only ice crystals and so appear white. On the other hand, cumulus clouds can be white from water vapor, but can grow dark if they fill with large water drops that eventually fall as rain. Nonprecipitating clouds can look dark as well if they are very thick and back lit by the sun. Clouds can give insight into what the weather is like and what's on the way. They're an important tool in weather forecasting. See the Cloudy Weather table on page 71 for some examples.

Cloudy Weather

Cumulus	Fluffy lower clouds that often "grow" during sunny days. Usually mean fair weather unless they grow tall late in the day.
Cirrostratus	Thin-layered high clouds of ice. Can mean that overcast skies or rain will follow.
Cirrus	High, wispy ice clouds. Often seen in clear skies and may mean fair weather will change to rain.
Altocumulus	Thick blue-gray, blanket-like clouds made of ice and water at middle heights. Rain or snow likely to follow, or at least cloudy skies.
Stratus	Flat layer of low clouds. Light rain, drizzle, or flurries likely.
Cumulonimbus	Giant thunderhead clouds that tower to high heights. Thunderstorms with heavy rain, hail, winds, and lightning are on the way.
Fog	Watery stratus clouds at ground level, especially common in the morning or evening. Morning fog often burns off with the sun by noon.

Track Cloudy Weather

Clouds are only one of the many factors—including fronts, winds, pressure systems, etc.—used to predict the weather. But clouds are one of the easiest to observe. You can use the information in the Cloud Types chart and Cloudy Weather table to identify clouds and made predictions about the weather on the way.

The anvil shape of this thunderhead identifies it as a cumulonimbus cloud.

Make a chart with these five headings: DATE/TIME, CLOUD TYPE, A.M. WEATHER, P.M. PREDICTED WEATHER, ACTUAL P.M. WEATHER (TIME). Fill in the chart every morning for a week, using the Cloud Types chart to identify the clouds and the Cloudy Weather table to make predictions. How accurate were your predictions?

Science Fair Spin

Design a similar experiment that investigates the connection between cloud types and front types. Use newspapers to track fronts and see if fronts were responsible for some of the cloud types you observe.

How Lightning Is Formed

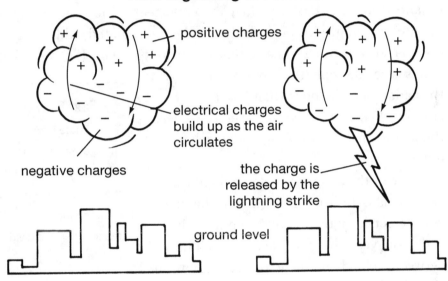

positive charges

electrical charges build up as the air circulates

negative charges

the charge is released by the lightning strike

ground level

Thunderstorms and Lightning

Storm Science

Our planet experiences as many as 50,000 thunderstorms every day. They are the world's most common kind of storm, bringing drenching rain, hail, lightning, and thunder, and sometimes spawning tornadoes (see page 98). In North America, most thunderstorms happen in the spring and summer. That's when air near the ground is warm but upper air is cold. These unstable air conditions spawn the giant anvil-shaped cumulonimbus clouds that produce thunderstorms. As the warm, moist air rises off the ground, as an updraft, it begins to cool. Once it reaches its dew-point temperature, a cloud begins to form. The condensation process that forms the cloud warms the air, allowing the cloud to continue to rise if conditions are right. This is how the tall, towering shape of a thunderhead develops.

Inside the cloud, updrafts keep pumping warm humid air into the storm, further fueling it. Meanwhile, some ice and water droplets grow large enough to fall out, dragging air down with them and creating downdrafts. The updrafts and downdrafts zoom up and down the cloud as fast as 5,000 feet (1,500 meters) per minute. Ice caught in the updrafts can be recirculated, adding layer upon layer until it's so heavy that it falls out as hail. If the surface winds reach 58 mph (93 kph) or faster—or if the hailstones are more than ¾ of an inch (2 cm) in diameter—it's declared a severe thunderstorm, and warning and watches are issued.

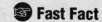 **Fast Fact**

To estimate how many miles are between lightning and you, count the number of seconds between the flash and the thunder and divide by five.

One of the dangerous elements of thunderstorms is lightning. Lightning happens when electricity travels between negatively and positively charged parts of a cloud or between a cloud and the ground. It's how an electrically charged cloud gets rid of—or dumps—its charge. Scientists think that a cloud becomes charged when various forms of upward- and downward-moving water and ice within the thunderhead collide with one another.

When a cloud discharges and lightning flashes, it heats the air to more than 43,000°F (24,000°C) along its path. That air expands and immediately contracts because the lightning is moving so fast—60,000 miles (96,000 km) per second. The quick expansion and contraction of the air creates sound waves, called thunder. Sound travels much slower than light, so we see the flash and then hear the thunder.

Lightning is dangerous. A bolt of lightning delivers thousands to millions of volts of electricity—enough to light up a town. About 500 people are struck by lightning a year in the United States. Around 100 of these strikes are fatal and many of the remaining victims are left with permanent injuries. Lightning strikes can result in brain damage, ruptured eardrums, and paralysis. Being "lightning smart" means paying attention when thunderstorm watches are issued, going indoors during storms, and staying away from tall trees, water, and high places if caught outside.

Lightning strikes both from cloud to cloud and from cloud to ground.

Static Sensor

Lightning happens when positive and negative charges build up in separate parts of storm clouds. This kind of build-up of extra charges is called static electricity. You experience small doses of static electricity when you walk across a carpet and then get zapped when touching a metal doorknob! The crackling sound that pulling clothes out of the dryer makes is static electricity, too. Lightning is simply static electricity on a much bigger scale. You can build an instrument to detect static electric charge in this activity.

You'll Need

- a dry day (humidity dampens static electricity)
- unsharpened pencil
- craft stick
- Scotch Magic cellophane tape (not all other kinds of clear tape work)
- balloon, blown up
- wool mitten, yarn, or hat
- masking tape
- pen or magic marker

1. Make a "T" with the craft stick, pencil, and masking tape as shown.

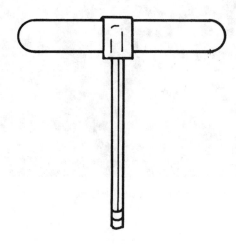

2. Tear off two 3-inch (7.5-cm) strips of cellophane tape and attach them to the edge of a desk or table so that they dangle.

3. Write a "-" (negative) symbol on the smooth side of one of the tape strips about midway down. Write "+" (positive) symbol on the other tape strip.

4. Stick the sticky side of the "+" strip of tape onto the smooth side of the "-" strip, as shown. Immediately and quickly peel them apart.

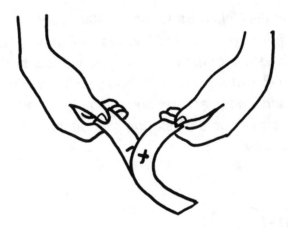

5. Stick one end of each tape strip onto an end of the craft stick so they dangle down, as shown. The strips' smooth and sticky sides should face the same way.

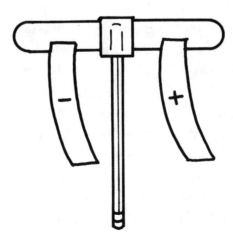

6. Your Static Sensor is ready! Use a balloon rubbed on hair or wool to test it. Computer or TV screens also test well. The strip of tape that moves forward toward the object indicates its charge—negative or positive. If neither strip moves, the object has no charge.

7. Test the charge of various objects and record your results on a chart. What conclusions can you draw from your findings?

Science Fair Spin

In the United States about 100 people are killed by lightning each year. Investigate lightning safety and create informative public-safety posters. You can also write and record radio public service announcements or direct and videotape TV public-service spots on staying safe during lightning storms.

Acid Rain

Rain, snow, or other precipitation that is polluted with acids is called **acid rain**. While normal rainwater is usually slightly acidic, certain air pollutants add dangerous amounts of acid to rainwater. Acid rain pollutes lakes, rivers, and streams and can kill fish and wildlife. Soil and forests are harmed by acid rain, and it also eats away at buildings, bridges, and statues.

Weather and the Environment

Acid rain is formed when the smoke and fumes from burning fossil fuels like oil, coal, and gasoline rise into the atmosphere and create sulfur dioxide and nitrogen oxide emissions. Up in the clouds, these pollutants react and form mild sulfuric and nitric acid solutions. When the clouds form precipitation—like snow or rain—the acids are carried with them back down to the earth. (Acids from pollutants that don't make it into clouds also fall back to the earth as dry particles or gases.) Because clouds can travel many hundreds of miles before "raining out" their acids, acid

This scientist is testing the water for acid rain.

rain can fall far from the factory or power plant that emitted the pollutants.

Acid rain affects both plant and animal life in land and water ecosystems. Trees exposed to acid rain—or dry-acid deposits—are weakened and can have stunted growth. Leaves "burned" by the acids are unable to photosynthesize food. Scientists also believe that acidic water harms soil. Lakes, streams, and ponds often take the brunt of acid rain because they not only collect the acid rain that falls directly into them, but also take in acid rain and dry-acid deposits that enter as rainwater runoff. The result can be disastrous—fish eggs and insect larvae won't hatch, the aquatic food web begins to disintegrate, and in very extreme cases the pond or lake will "die."

Since the 1980s, when studies strongly pointed to industrial emissions as the main source of acid rain, countries have attempted to clean up their air. In the United States, the 1990 amendments to the Clean Air Act required power plants and factories to burn cleaner fuel to reduce pollutants that produce acid rain.

> 🐾 **Fast Fact**
> One of the most acidic lakes on record is Little Echo Pond in Franklin, New York, with a pH of 4.2—about the same acidity as a tomato. Unpolluted lakes and streams have a pH around 6.5. (A lower pH value indicates higher acidity.)

Testing for Trouble

Acid rain is caused by acidic pollutants released into the air by cars, trucks, factories, and power plants. In this activity you can make an acid-base test solution and then use it to test your rainwater for acidity.

You'll Need
- medium-sized red cabbage
- one quart (950 ml) distilled water
- knife
- pan with lid
- stove or microwave oven
- strainer
- vinegar

- baking soda
- collected rainwater
- large glass jar
- measuring cups
- 4 glasses or jars (need to hold at least 12 oz. [355 ml])
- tablespoon

1. Wash and pat dry a red cabbage and then cut it up. Fill a pan with a quart (950 ml) of distilled water. Place the pieces of cabbage in the pan of water, cover it, and let it simmer for about 30 minutes. (You can also cook it in a microwave for about 15 minutes instead.)

2. Set the pan aside and let it cool. Then strain the 2–3 cups (470–710 ml) of cabbage juice into a glass jar. This is your acid/base testing solution.

3. Label the four glasses: NEUTRAL, RAIN, ACID, BASE.

4. Fill the RAIN glass with 1 cup (240 ml) of rainwater and set it aside.

5. Fill the other three glasses with 1 cup (240 ml) of distilled water. Add a tablespoon (15 ml) of vinegar to the ACID glass and a tablespoon (15 ml) of baking soda to the BASE glass. Add nothing to the NEUTRAL glass.

6. Pour in 1/4 cup (60 ml) of the testing solution into these three glasses. The testing solution should turn the ACID red, the BASE blue, and the NEUTRAL should be the unchanged color of the test solution (watered-down purple).

7. Now you're ready to test your rainwater. Pour 1/4 cup (60 ml) of the testing solution into the RAIN glass. Is your rainwater acidic, basic, or neutral?

Science Fair Spin

Investigate the effects of acid rain on plant growth. Use two identical plants, such as bean seedlings or cuttings from a philodendron. Water each plant equally, but give one distilled water and the other acidic water. (Add 1 tsp. [5 ml] vinegar to 2 cups [470 ml] of water to make acidic water). Chart their growth over a number of weeks.

Storm Photographer

Cool Weather Careers

Warren Faidley is the world's first full-time, professional storm photographer. His award-winning photographs have appeared in magazines, newspapers, and books. He was a consultant for the blockbuster tornado movie *Twister*, too. Faidley stalks and shoots about 100 storms a year—Midwest tornadoes in the spring, Southwest lightning storms in the summer, and Atlantic hurricanes in the late summer and fall.

Photographing lightning and snapping hurricane images can be treacherous at times. "Lightning that hit near me launched my career," says Faidley. He was taking pictures in Arizona when a lightning bolt struck a light pole only 400 feet (120 m) away. The flash blinded him and he fell down an embankment—but the photograph made *Life* magazine. Faidley has a vehicle outfitted with communications, computer, and weather-forecasting equipment to help him find photogenic storms and weather. Though not a trained meteorologist—he studied journalism during college—Faidley has learned a lot about how to use weather data to forecast what's on the way. "We do most of our own forecasting because we're looking for specific storms in a very targeted area," he explains. "We use the same things as the weather service—dew point, winds, and barometric pressure."

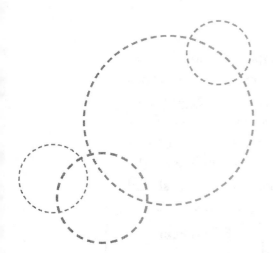

Why the Winds Blow

Wind is air on the move. Winds can vary from a gentle breeze to a hurricane gale, but all wind results from temperature differences in the atmosphere. Air is heated from the ocean or land beneath it. The sun unevenly heats the surface, which causes uneven heating of the air above. The equator heats up more than the North Pole, for example. Surface temperatures and the air above them depend on latitude, season, and geographical features like mountains or oceans. Air above warm areas expands and rises, and cooler air flows in to replace it. That rising and flowing air is wind.

Warm air continually rising over the equator and being replaced by cooler air moving in from higher latitudes creates global or prevailing winds. These winds are responsible for the general circulation of the atmosphere. If the earth stood still, these winds would blow in a straight line. But our planet is spinning, so global winds are turned as they blow. This curving pattern is the Coriolis effect. The atmosphere's general circulation combines with the Coriolis effect to produce the north and south polar easterly winds, the prevailing westerlies at the mid-latitudes, and the northeast and southwest trade winds on both sides of the equator (see diagram below). The strongest westerlies occur at heights of 6 to 12 miles (10 to 20 km) and are concentrated in narrow channels of fast-moving upper atmospheric air called jet streams. Jet streams in both hemispheres usually follow the boundaries between cold and warm air and can exceed 200 mph (320 kmh).

All winds are named for the direction from which they blow. The northeast trade winds in the northern hemisphere come from the east and north and blow toward the west,

> ### 🐾 Fast Fact
>
> The strongest nontornado wind ever measured on the earth's surface was 225 mph (362 km per hour). It was recorded on Mount Washington in New Hampshire on April 12, 1934.

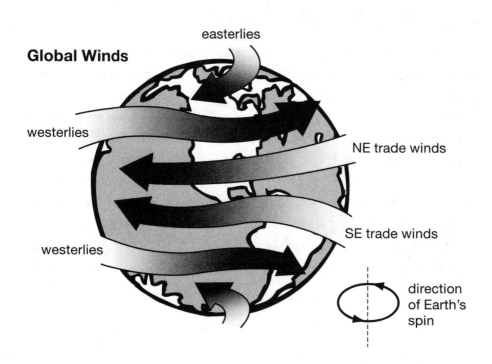

Global Winds

easterlies

westerlies

NE trade winds

SE trade winds

westerlies

direction of Earth's spin

for example. The exact position of prevailing winds and jet streams change throughout the year. They sometimes shift a bit from one year to the next, but they are major permanent forces in determining the climates of the planet.

Smaller-Scale Winds

Within the general circulation of the earth's atmosphere caused by the prevailing winds are smaller-scale winds. Whereas prevailing winds play an important part in determining the climate of an area, smaller-scale winds drive day-to-day weather. These synoptic-scale winds are air moving around small areas of high and low pressure in the atmosphere. Air flows in toward a low-pressure area (low). Because of the Coriolis effect, that means winds blow counterclockwise around a low. Alternately, air flows away from a high-pressure area (high). Therefore winds blow clockwise around a high. This means that if you stand with your back to the wind in the northern hemisphere, it's likely that a low-pressure area is at your left and a high-pressure area at your right.

Local winds are winds that blow only in a specific place. Sea or lake breezes between land and water are a common type of local wind. Land heats and cools faster than water. This means that warm air over land rises, and cooler air over the ocean or a lake blows in to replace it during the day. The reverse can happen at night as the land cools faster than the water. Mountains can create a similar situation as high mountain slopes heat up. The rising warm air above them pulls cooler air up from the valleys. As the slopes cool at night, the heavy cool air sinks and flows down into the valley.

> **👉 Fast Fact**
>
> People around the world have given their local winds individual names. In India, a down-valley wind is called a *dadur*. A sandstorm wind is called a *haboob* in Sudan. And a *chinook* wind is a warm, dry wind in the western United States.

Reading the Wind

In 1805, a British naval admiral named Sir Francis Beaufort invented a wind-measuring scale based on observations of waves and ship's sails. Wind strengths were divided into 13 categories called forces. This Beaufort Scale was later adapted for land use and is still used today to estimate wind speeds. You can use this handy scale to estimate wind speeds in your area, too.

Study the Beaufort Wind Scale below and on the next page. Create a chart with the following headings: DATE/TIME, WIND OBSERVATIONS, BEAUFORT SCALE. Use the chart to note your observations of the wind and use them to determine a Beaufort Scale rating.

Design an experiment that tests the accuracy of the Beaufort Scale and/or compares it to the accuracy of the anemometer on page 89.

Science Fair Spin

The Beaufort Wind Scale

Beaufort Number	Kind of Wind	Wind Speed	Effects of Wind
0	calm	less than 1 mph (or 1 km/h)	Air feels still. Smoke rises straight up. Weather or wind vane doesn't move.
1	light air	1–3 mph (1–5 km/h)	Smoke drifts a little as it rises. Weather vane doesn't move.
2	light breeze	4–7 mph (6–11 km/h)	Can feel wind on face. Smoke follows wind. Leaves rustle. Flags stir. Weather vanes move.

Beaufort Number	Kind of Wind	Wind Speed	Effects of Wind
3	gentle breeze	8–12 mph (12–19 km/h)	Leaves and twigs move constantly. Light flags extend.
4	moderate breeze	13–18 mph (20–28 km/h)	Dust, loose paper, and leaves blow about. Thin tree branches sway. Flags flap.
5	fresh breeze	19–24 mph (29–38 km/h)	Small trees sway. Small waves crest on lakes and streams. Flags ripple.
6	strong breeze	25–31 mph (39–49 km/h)	Thick tree branches sway constantly. Flags beat. Umbrellas turn inside out.
7	moderate gale	32–38 mph (50–61 km/h)	Big trees sway. The wind pushes when walking against it. Flags extend completely.
8	fresh gale	39–46 mph (62–74 km/h)	Twigs are torn off trees. Walking against wind is difficult.
9	strong gale	47–54 mph (75–88 km/h)	Slight building damage—antennas and shingles blow off and awnings rip. Tree branches break.
10	whole gale	55–63 mph (89–102 km/h)	Trees snap or are uprooted. Buildings are damaged.
11	storm	64–73 mph (103–117 km/h)	Widespread building damage. Cars overturn, trees uproot or snap and blow away.
12	hurricane	74+ mph (118+ km/h)	Violent destruction and widespread damage. Buildings are destroyed.

What's the Beaufort Scale wind rating of the wind here?

The Anemometer

An anemometer is an instrument designed to measure wind speed. The earliest kind of wind-speed measurer was probably the pressure anemometer. It has a hanging plate along a curved scale that the wind forces higher as its strength increases. Similar wind gauges use metal balls on swinging arms or tethers to measure wind.

The most commonly used anemometers in weather stations today are rotation anemometers. These instruments consist of three or four cone-shaped cups attached to short rods that are connected at right angles to a vertical shaft. As the wind blows, the cups are pushed, which turns the shaft. The number of turns per minute is usually translated into wind speed by a system of gears leading to a readout.

Researchers who need very precise wind measurements often use hot-wire anemometers, which measure the amount of electric current needed to keep a hot wire at a constant temperature as the wind blows on it. Another sophisticated type of anemometer is the acoustic anemometer. It works on the principle that the speed of a sound signal is affected by wind speed.

Anemometer

**Build a
Weather
Station**

You can measure wind speed by making and using this pressure-type anemometer.

You'll Need

► large protractor
► Ping-Pong ball
► tape
► 12-inch (30-cm) length of strong thread or fishing line

1. Tape one end of the thread to the Ping-Pong ball and the other end to the center point on the base of the protractor.

2. Hold your anemometer level, with the base of the protractor up, and make sure that the ball swings freely.

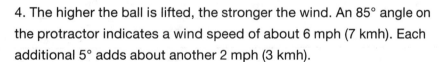

3. To measure the wind, stand facing into the wind and hold the anemometer away from your body. The wind lifts the Ping-Pong ball, moving the thread along the protractor's scale. The thread's height along the scale indicates the speed. The ball should move in a smooth upward lift. If it's moving away from the gauge, move to stand more directly into the wind.

4. The higher the ball is lifted, the stronger the wind. An 85° angle on the protractor indicates a wind speed of about 6 mph (7 kmh). Each additional 5° adds about another 2 mph (3 kmh).

Science Fair Spin

The Aztecs measured wind with a tripod set up over concentric walled rings. Wind was measured by dropping balls from the tripod and noting in which ring they fell. The stronger the winds, the farther out into the rings the balls would fall. Invent a wind-measuring device of your own.

Feeling the Chill

Wind can make cold temperatures feel even colder. That's because the wind blows away the normal layer of warmed air covering human skin. The heat escapes, and you feel colder. The faster the wind, the faster the heat is carried away, and the colder it feels. The temperature of the air isn't really colder when the wind blows. You just feel colder. This is called the wind chill index or factor. It's a temperature that represents how cold it feels.

Discover the chilling difference wind makes for yourself. Study the wind chill chart below. The actual air temperature runs across the top. Wind speed is down the left side. The wind chill temperature is found by intersecting the two. Which feels colder: A 30°F (-1°C) day with no wind, or a 50°F (10°C) day with 25 mph (40 kmh) winds?

Wind Chill Chart

Actual Thermometer Readings (°F)

Wind Speed (mph)	50	40	30	20	10	0	-10	-20	-30	-40
					Wind Chill Temperatures (°F)					
0	50	40	30	20	10	0	-10	-20	-30	-40
5	48	37	27	16	6	-5	-15	-26	-36	-47
10	40	28	16	4	-9	-21	-33	-46	-58	-70
15	36	22	9	-5	-18	-36	-45	-58	-72	-85
20	32	18	4	-10	-25	-39	-53	-67	-82	-96
25	30	16	0	-15	-29	-44	-59	-74	-88	-104
30	28	13	-2	-18	-33	-48	-63	-79	-94	-109
35	27	11	-4	-20	-35	-49	-67	-82	-98	-113
40	26	10	-6	-21	-37	-53	-69	-85	-100	-116

Wind Vane

Build a Weather Station

Knowing which way the wind is blowing is an important part of weather forecasting. People have been monitoring the direction of winds for thousands of years, and the wind vane—or weather vane—is probably the oldest of all meteorological instruments. Make your own wind vane and track the direction of winds over time.

You'll Need

- heavy cardboard or Styrofoam food tray or egg carton lid
- unsharpened pencil
- pen cap that fits loosely over pencil end
- scissors
- heavy waterproof tape
- compass (optional)
- glue
- empty soup can
- sand or fine gravel
- modeling clay
- clear contact paper or laminating film (optional)

1. Trace or photocopy the wind pointer pattern on page 92. Trace the pattern onto heavy cardboard or Styrofoam and then cut it out. (You can waterproof a cardboard wind pointer by covering it with laminating film or contact paper.)

2. Trace or photocopy the round direction disk on page 92 and glue it onto cardboard, paperboard, or Styrofoam. Laminate it if desired, or you can make it fairly waterproof just by covering it with plastic wrap and taping the plastic wrap to the bottom. Poke a hole in the center of the disk where the dot is. The hole needs to be big enough for a pencil to fit through.

3. Push the pencil, eraser-side down, through the hole in the direction disk. Stick the eraser end into a small ball of clay and set it in the bottom of a can and fill with sand or gravel. This will make it stable.

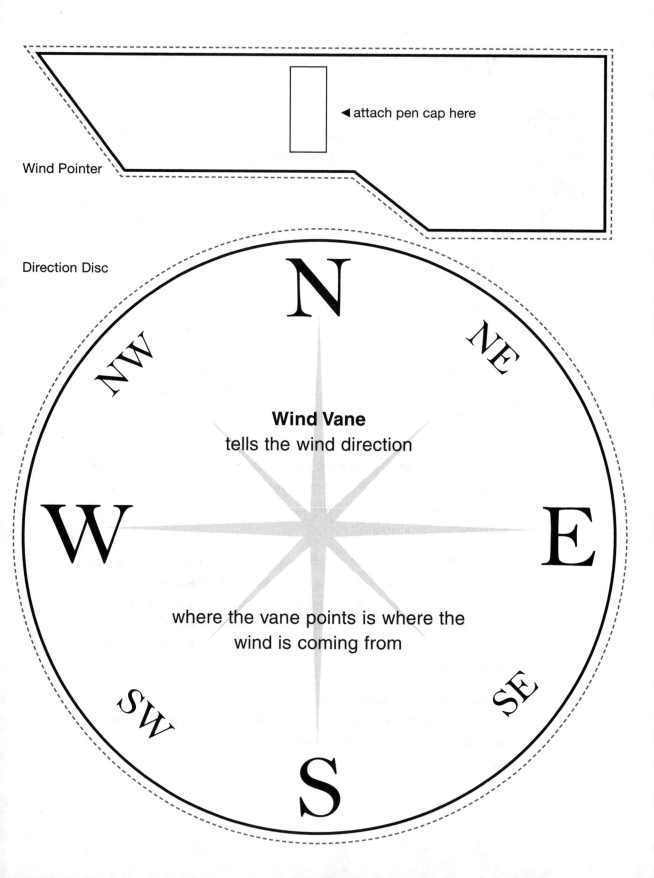

◄ attach pen cap here

Wind Pointer

Direction Disc

N

NW

NE

Wind Vane
tells the wind direction

W

E

where the vane points is where the
wind is coming from

SW

SE

S

4. Tape the pen cap onto one side of the wind pointer. (Use its pattern as a guide to where to place it.)

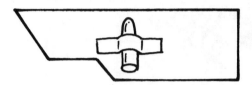

5. Set the wind pointer on top of the pencil by fitting the pen cap over the unsharpened pencil end. Make sure the pointer is level and if not, re-tape the pen cap. Also give the pointer a spin to make sure it moves freely. If it doesn't, you'll need to use a different kind of pen cap.

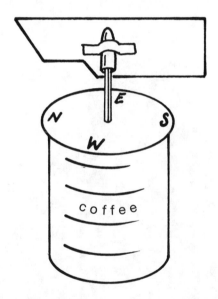

6. Your wind vane is ready! Place it outside in an open area at least two feet above ground and away from high walls and tall trees. Use a compass—or the sun—to set "North" on the direction disk toward north. The wind pointer's narrow end will swing into the wind, indicating the way the wind is coming from. If the pointer is pointing to the west, the wind is blowing from the west and is called a westerly wind.

This wind vane points a cow into the wind.

The Power of Wind

Wind is moving air, and moving air has the power to move! Sailboats, windmills, and kites are all examples of how we use the power of wind. In this activity you can measure the lifting power of your own wind source—breath.

You'll Need

- ► scissors
- ► pushpin
- ► unsharpened pencil
- ► small paper cup
- ► tape

- ► heavy thread
- ► small objects like coins, marbles, erasers, paper clips, etc.

1. Trace or photocopy the pinwheel pattern below and cut along all its dashed lines.

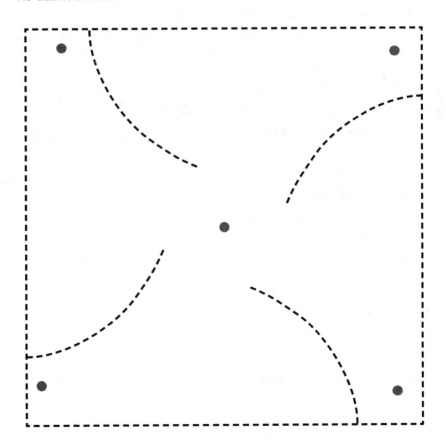

2. Hold the pinwheel pattern up to the light or against a window and trace the middle dot onto the back.

3. Set the pattern face down on a notebook. Carefully bend—but don't crease—the pinwheel "arms" inward one at a time, as shown. Once all the dots are piled on top of each other over the center dot, push the pushpin through.

4. Attach the assembled pinwheel onto the end of a pencil by pushing the pushpin into the end of the eraser as far as it will go.

5. Tape one end of a 12-inch (30-cm) piece of heavy thread to the middle of the pencil and the other end to the outside of a paper cup.

6. Loosely hold the pencil between your index and middle fingers and blow on the pinwheel to make it spin. Practice this for a while, noticing how the thread wraps around the pencil. (If the pinwheel is spinning but the pencil isn't turning, try pushing the pushpin farther into the eraser.)

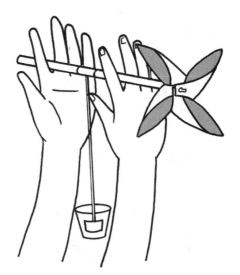

7. Place a small object in the cup. Blow a single breath (wind gust) and count how many times the thread wraps around the pencil, like you did in step 6. Repeat this with other objects, jotting down the number of pencil wraps each breath powered for each object. Can you infer and rank the

comparative weight of their tested objects based on the number of string wraps? What was heaviest? Lightest?

Create a number of different pinwheel designs and test them for their lifting power.

**Science Fair
Spin**

Worldly Wind Poems

The people of the world have named local winds for centuries. Below is a list of 10 local winds from around the world, where they blow, and a description of the wind. Write a poem about one or more of these unique winds. Many of the wind names made good acrostic poems, using the letter of the wind name to start each line. Try to include something about the wind's origin and characteristics into the poem and consider illustrating it as well.

Worldly Winds

Wind Name	Where It Blows	What It's Like
zonda	Argentina	hot, dry, westerly
purga	Russia, Siberia	cold, blizzards, northeasterly
angin-laut	Malaysia	breeze from the sea
haboob	Sudan	sandstorm or dust storm
kona	Hawaii	southwesterly, brings rain
chinook	Western United States and Canada	dry, warm, westerly wind
dadur	Ganges Valley of India	down-valley wind
helm	Eden Valley of Northern England	cold, northeasterly
junk	Vietnam	southerly or southeasterly monsoon wind
khamsin	Egypt	desert wind, southerly

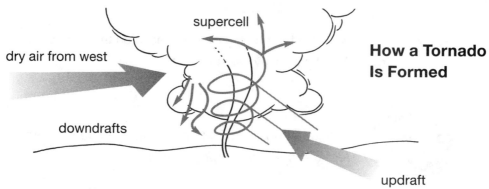

dry air from west

supercell

How a Tornado Is Formed

downdrafts

updraft

Tornadoes

Tornadoes are the most violent storms on earth. Their funnel shape is a swirling vortex of spinning air. The largest tornadoes can have winds as fast as 300 mph (480 kmh), the fastest winds on the planet's surface. Winds of this intensity can lift trains and trucks, smash houses, and make flying missiles out of cars. Tornadoes are intense storms that do millions of dollars of damage and kill dozens of people each year in North America. But most are short-lived and confined to small areas. The average tornado lasts only a few minutes and travels less than a mile.

Storm Science

> 🌀 **Fast Fact**
>
> The deadliest tornado in U.S. history plowed though Missouri, Illinois, and Indiana on March 18, 1925. It killed 689 people and injured more than 2,000.

Thunderstorms spawn tornadoes. Small thunderstorms can throw out F0 to F2 tornadoes (see scale on pages 99 and 100). But the biggest twisters come from supercell storms— giant towering cumulonimbus thunderstorms that soar toward the stratosphere and are many miles in diameter. These storms are common in the Great Plains states in the spring, and it's no coincidence that Tornado Alley runs from Iowa to Texas.

Supercell storms form as warm, moist air from the Gulf of Mexico moves north. As that air begins to rise, it encounters unstable air and winds of different speeds as it climbs and condenses into a towering thunderhead cloud. These variable winds in the growing thunderstorm set some of the air in the storm spinning horizontally. Updrafts in the storm tilt this tube of spinning air on its end, creating what's called a **mesocyclone**. A mesocyclone is a rotating column of air inside a thunderstorm and provides the vertical spin that tornadoes need. Just exactly how a piece of that vertical spin tightens, speeds up, and drops out of the cloud as a tornado isn't yet completely understood by scientists.

Tornadoes often topple trees onto homes, cars, barns, and sheds.

Fujita Tornado Scale

Fujita Number	Wind Speed	Observed Damage
F0	40–72 mph 64–116 km/h	**Light.** Knocked-over chimneys and billboards, broken branches.
F1	73–112 mph 117–180 km/h	**Moderate.** Roof and garage damage, mobile homes moved.
F2	113–157 mph 181–253 km/h	**Significant.** Trees snapped, roofs torn off, boxcars overturned.
F3	158–206 mph 254–332 km/h	**Severe.** Trees uprooted, cars lifted and tossed, trains overturned.

continued on next page

Fujita Tornado Scale (continued)

Fujita Number	Wind Speed	Observed Damage
F4	207–260 mph 333–418 km/h	**Devastating.** Well-built homes leveled, cars became missiles.
F5	261–318 mph 419–512 km/h	**Incredible.** Strong homes lifted off foundations and destroyed, steel-reinforced concrete structures badly damaged.

The instruments on the tower of this severe-weather station give wind direction and speed. The tank on the left is a rain gauge, and the white box on the right houses thermometers, barometers, and psychrometers.

Tornado in a Bottle

Tornadoes are whirling vortexes of spinning air. In this activity, you can make a similar vortex of spinning water.

You'll Need
▶ 2 one-liter or two-liter clear plastic bottles
▶ duct tape
▶ water
▶ food coloring

1. Fill one of the bottles about three-quarters full of water. Add a few drops of food coloring.

2. Set the other bottle on top of the first bottle and tape them together with the duct tape.

3. Carefully turn the bottles over so the full bottle is on top. Hold one hand firmly on the bottom bottle. Use your other hand to swirl the top bottle in a circle. A vortex is created.

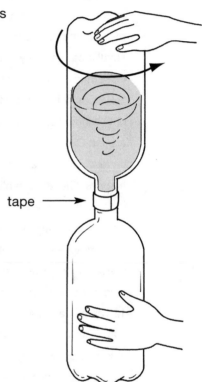

tape →

Science Fair Spin

Investigate the history of tornadoes in your town. What is the current safety protocol for such severe weather?

Tornado Chaser

Cool Weather Careers

Howard Bluestein is a university professor and research meteorologist with a passion for chasing tornadoes. "To me, the tornado is one of meteorology's last frontiers," says Bluestein. Why and exactly how some thunderstorms spawn twisters is still not completely understood. "Tornadoes are very difficult to study because it's so hard to make measurements," he explains. "They don't last long, they encompass a small area, and they're difficult to predict." That's why he uses an up-close-and-personal method to collect data and study tornadoes.

Bluestein and his "storm chasing" graduate students at the University of Oklahoma spend April through June driving thousands of miles around Oklahoma, Texas, and Kansas chasing down tornadoes. "It would be fascinating to actually get inside the tornado and take a look around," he says. "Since we can't, we try to get close enough to aim our portable radar unit and measure the wind field in and around the tornado. That information helps us to learn more about how twisters form."

Tornadoes and other severe weather have fascinated this storm chaser since a twister hit near his home in Massachusetts when he was a small boy. He was also interested in astronomy and electronics and at 12 years of age became a licensed amateur radio operator—something many storm watchers have in common. As a college student Bluestein studied electrical engineering, but a professor inspired him to switch to meteorology. He has been studying tornadoes ever since. He figures that over the past 20 years he's seen more than 100. One especially fierce twister that Bluestein was chasing in April 1991 had winds of 280 mph (448 kph). It was the first F5 tornado to have its winds officially recorded (not estimated). It also came a little too close for comfort. "The tornado leaped across the road right in front of us," recalls Bluestein. "You could see its furious spin. It was very, very clear."

This tornado plowed its way past storm chasers in Cordell, Oklahoma.

Air Pollution and Thermal Inversions

In general, air temperature decreases as altitude increases. It's colder on a mountaintop than down in the valley, for example. This

Weather and the Environment

fact guarantees mixing of the atmosphere because the low warm air rises, then cools as it reaches high altitudes and sinks, and is then warmed and rises again.

However, sometimes a layer of warm air stalls over a layer of cooler air and becomes trapped. This is called a **thermal inversion**. The cooler air close to the ground is trapped because it is heavier than the warm air above it. Inversions are common and don't last very long. But inversions that do last worsen the build-up of air pollution from factories, cars, power plants, and trucks. An inversion keeps the polluted air down near the surface, preventing winds from mixing it into the atmosphere where it can be diluted.

What atmospheric conditions produce thermal inversions? Stationary high-pressure systems with mild winds can cause an inversion at the surface. But sometimes they are caused simply by nighttime surface cooling in an area. This is especially true where the air is free of clouds, which hold in heat like a blanket. These nighttime inversions usually break up when the next day's sun heats things up. But a region's geographical features can make it extra prone to inversions. Southern California has inversions nearly 55 percent of the time due to a semi-permanent high-pressure area off its coast. These inversions make the region's air pollution problem even worse. Inversions are also more common during the winter and in colder climates when the surface loses more heat than it gains.

Within days, the atmospheric mixing stopped by an inversion can lead to hazardous concentrations of pollutants. An inversion over Donora, Pennsylvania, in 1948 led to the deaths of 20 people and respiratory illness in thousands. The severity of the chemical-spill disaster at Bhopal, India, in 1984 that killed at least 3,300 people was due in part to a thermal inversion that concentrated the lethal chemical near the earth's surface.

Weather is only part of the pollution equation. Many other factors influence the quality of a region's air. In the United States the Environmental Protection Agency (EPA) has developed the Pollutant Standards Index (PSI). It's a uniform way of measuring the levels of five major pollutants: particulate matter (soot, dust, and other particles), sulfur dioxide, carbon monoxide, nitrogen dioxide, and ground-level ozone (not stratospheric ozone needed to sustain the ozone layer). The EPA has standard and unacceptable levels for all these pollutants. The concentrations of all these pollutants are converted into a PSI number from 0 to 500 (see the table on page 105). All towns with more than 200,000 people are given a daily PSI. PSI levels in the United States usually fall between 0 and 100.

The Pollutant Standards Index

Index Value	PSI Descriptor	Cautionary Statements
0–50	good	None required.
51–100	moderate	None required.
101–200	unhealthful	Persons with existing heart or respiratory ailments should reduce physical exertion and outdoor activity. The general population should reduce vigorous outdoor activity.
201–300	very unhealthful	The elderly and persons with existing heart or lung disease should stay indoors and reduce physical activity. General population should avoid vigorous outdoor activity.
301+	hazardous	The elderly and persons with existing diseases should stay indoors and avoid physical exertion. At PSI levels above 400, everyone should remain indoors and keep windows and doors closed.

Inverting Air

Thermal inversions greatly increase pollution by trapping pollutants near the surface and preventing atmospheric mixing. In this activity you can see how warm air traps cold air beneath it during an inversion.

You'll Need
▶ 2 identical glass jars
▶ incense
▶ piece of thin cardboard or poster board
▶ black paper
▶ lamp
▶ grease pencil, permanent marker, or crayon

1. Set a lamp near a dark background, like black paper taped over a stack of books.

2. Set one of the glass jars upside down and write WARM on it. Set the other jar right side up and write COLD on it.

3. Fill the COLD jar with smoke by holding it upside down over burning incense. Quickly cover the jar with the piece of cardboard.

4. Cool the air in the jar. Either set the jar in a freezer or in a bowl of ice. Be careful not to let out the smoke!

5. Heat the air in the WARM jar. You can set the jar on a radiator or in an oven for a few minutes. Or pour hot water into the jar, dump it out, and dry it thoroughly.

6. Take the COLD jar out of the freezer and set in front of the dark background so the smoke is clearly visible. Then turn the WARM jar upside down and set it directly on top of the COLD jar. Immediately slide the cardboard out. Why does the smoky air stay down in the bottom COLD jar? What's trapping it?

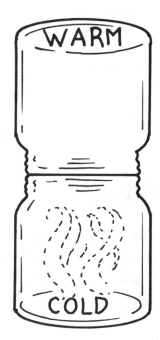

7. Carefully turn both jars over so the warm air is at the bottom and the cold air at the top. Watch the wind blow!

Science Fair Spin

Most newspapers report a daily Pollutant Standards Index in the weather section. Sometimes it's called an air quality index or an air pollution index. (But don't confuse it with the mold/pollen count.) Track the pollution level in your city over a week. Can you link higher air pollution to weather trends like temperature or fronts?

Trap Pollution Particles

Here's an activity that will let you investigate the amount of particulate (soot, dust, and other particles) air pollution in your area.

You'll Need
- ▶ light-colored masking or double-sided tape
- ▶ index cards
- ▶ magnifying lens

1. Stick loops of light-colored masking or double-sided tape on index cards. Cover as much of the index card as you can, and cover each index card equally.

2. Use more tape to stick your cards to walls, posts, and other structures, both inside and outside.

3. After a few days retrieve the cards. Use the magnifying lens to observe what particles have collected on the sticky surfaces. How do the cards left in different places compare?

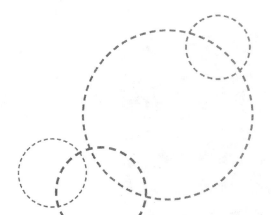

Weather Watching and Forecasting

Everyone likes to watch, talk about, and try to predict the weather. The weather influences more than just what to wear or whether a picnic is canceled. Weather can also make or break a harvest or bring about a heating-fuel shortage. And severe weather can cause widespread destruction and even death.

People have been observing wind, rain, cloud, and temperature patterns throughout history in an attempt to predict the weather. All cultures are filled with weather folklore and sayings like "Red sky at night, sailors delight. Red sky at morning, sailors take warning" that are a testament to humankind's interest in weather watching and forecasting. Even in modern times, people still use simple instruments, some basic knowledge, and keen observations to pre-

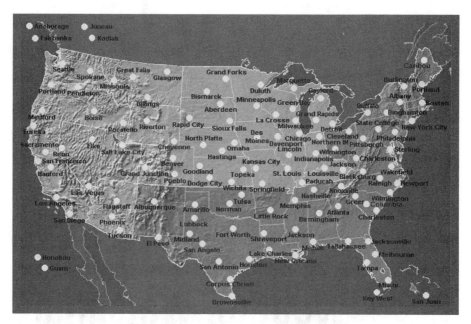

Each of these white dots represents a forecasting office of the National Weather Service.

dict unfolding local weather conditions for themselves. Knowing simply the wind direction and cloud types can tell you a lot about what weather is right around the corner.

High-Tech Weather Watchers

Scientists with the job of forecasting detailed weather conditions for large regions over many days need a sophisticated array of high-tech equipment. Weather stations measure and record the same weather conditions discussed in this book: temperature, barometric pressure, humidity, wind speed, and wind direction. Professional weather stations, however, use more sophisticated instruments to record local ground-level conditions and transmit them from thousands of positions to central forecasting offices. Aircraft collect information about upper-level winds while ships and buoys provide data about the weather above oceans.

This weather satellite is almost ready for launch.

Weather balloons measure temperature, humidity, and pressure at different heights in the atmosphere. About 800 weather-observation stations around the world each launch two weather balloons per day. The helium-filled balloons carry instruments that collect and transmit weather data (called radiosondes) until they reach a height where they burst and parachute back to the ground. Satellites are another important weather-gathering tool. Their images of the globe allow scientists to see clouds from above and to spot storms and hurricanes developing over the oceans. Satellites also provide temperatures of cloud-tops, the upper atmosphere, and the oceans, as well as wind speeds and the location of otherwise invisible water vapor. Weather satellites are either polar orbiting or geostationary. Polar orbiting satellites orbit at about 530 miles (850 km) above the earth. Because the earth rotates underneath their orbit, these satellites image a different section with every pass. Geostationary satellites orbit at a much higher 22,400 miles (36,000 km) above the planet. They move in sync with the earth's rotation at a fixed place on the equator. But because geostationary satellites have such a high orbit, they take pictures covering a wide area. Four properly positioned geostationary satellites can cover the whole earth at once.

 Fast Fact

The supercomputer at the National Meteorological Center can handle about two billion weather-tracking operations per second.

Radar has been used since World War II to show where rain, snow, hail, or other precipitation is falling. Radar works by sending out radio waves and analyzing their returning echoes to determine what they bounced off of. Doppler radar is a new and improved type of radar that not only measures precipitation but also shows wind speed and direction, which meteorologists can use to better map the boundaries between fronts. Doppler radar is part of the NEXRAD (Next Generation Weather Radar) network of more than 100 radar units mostly operated by the National Weather Service in the United States.

A Doppler radar tower.

Mapping out a Forecast

Much of the improvement in weather forecasting over the past 30 years is thanks to number-crunching computers. Without them forecasts of more than a few hours would be impossible. Weather data like temperature, pressure, wind, and humidity are collected from satellites, weather stations, radar, etc. This data is continually fed into computers that make a grid of weather conditions covering the whole planet from the sea into the stratosphere. The computer uses mathematical equations to project how the conditions will change over time and make forecasts. The current data is also displayed in what's called a **synoptic chart**, or weather map. Professional weather maps often use complicated symbols, but simplified weather maps appear in nearly every newspaper and help the public understand the weather.

Even with radar, satellites, and super-computers, weather forecasting has its limits. The National Weather Service issues short-range forecasts and extended forecasts. Short-range forecasts predict the weather over the next 18 to 36 hours with good accuracy. Extended forecasts usually predict the weather over the next five days and are less reliable. Daily temperature forecasts for three to five days ahead are more likely to be accurate than predictions of precipitation because the conditions that determine precipitation are complex. And while major front movement can be forecast days ahead of time, pinpointing when the local thunderstorms or snowstorms brought by those fronts will hit is much more difficult. Even with inevitable improvements in weather-collecting instruments and more understanding of atmospheric phenomena, many scientists doubt that accurate weather forecasts of more than two weeks ahead will ever be possible. The weather is dependent on too many interrelated and unpredictable factors.

 Fast Fact

More than 3,500 weather stations around the world take hourly measurements of temperature, air pressure, wind direction and speed, humidity, rainfall, and other conditions and transmit the information to forecasting centers.

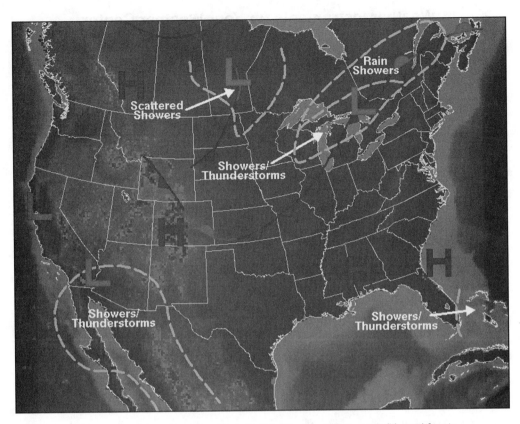

This weather map shows high-pressure areas (H), low-pressure areas (L), and fronts.

Put It All Together!

Build a Weather Station

Set up all the weather instruments created throughout this book as a weather station and record and track the changes in weather over a week, or longer.

You'll Need
▶ rain gauge (page 57)
▶ barometer (page 10)
▶ thermometer (page 35)
▶ psychrometer (page 66)
▶ anemometer (page 89)
▶ wind vane (page 91)
▶ paper and pencil

Weather Instruments for Your Weather Center

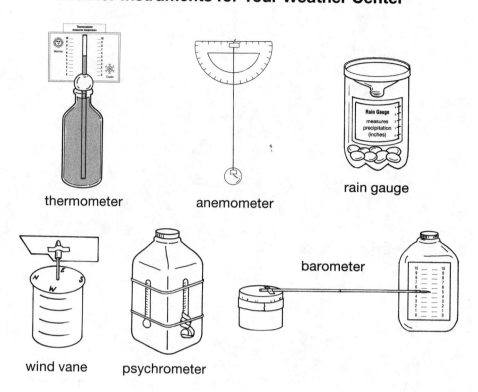

thermometer   anemometer

rain gauge

wind vane   psychrometer

barometer

1. Set up the rain gauge, thermometer, psychrometer, anemometer, and wind vane outside. (Note: Consider taking the thermometer and wind vane out in the morning and bringing them back in every afternoon—they'll hold up better that way. Remember that the rain gauge must be reset to "0" each day.) Set up the barometer inside.

2. Create a weather-tracking chart to record your data. Here's an example of what to include:

Date/Time _____

Precipitation	Wind
What kind? _____	Direction _____
How much? _____	Speed _____

continued on page 118

This weather station houses instruments to read temperature, air pressure, and relative humidity. A weather observer comes and takes the readings.

Humidity	Temperature
Wet-bulb temp _____	Reading _____
Dry-bulb temp _____	Hot, warm, cool, or cold? _____
Relative humidity _____	Rising or falling? _____

Air Pressure	Anything Interesting?
Reading _____	_____
Rising or falling? _____	_____

Clouds	
Cover: partly, half, mostly, or	_____
totally? _____	_____
Kinds? _____	_____

3. Take weather readings each day, or even once in the morning and once in the afternoon. Use the cloud types diagram on page 68 to help you identify clouds. Use the chart on page 67 to calculate relative humidity.

Science Fair Spin

After a week of weather data collecting, create a chart that combines all of the readings. Then compare it to "real" weather reports from the week's newspapers or weather Web sites. Which instruments performed best?

This roadside weather station is automated. It radios its weather readings to a forecasting office and is powered by a solar panel.

Test a Forecast

How accurate are long- and short-term forecasts in your area? Find out in this activity. Collect the published five-day forecast for your town from a local newspaper or weather Web site every day for five days in a row (Monday through Friday). Order the five forecasts in chronological order and see how accurate they were. Did the Monday forecast of Friday's weather (a five-day forecast) actually happen? How about the Tuesday prediction for Wednesday's weather (a one-day forecast)? Was the temperature or precipitation predicated more likely to happen?

Mapping It Out

Weather maps aren't just for meteorologists anymore! Newspapers, television news, and the Internet are all common sources of weather maps. You can practice reading and understanding weather maps in this activity.

Collect a week's worth of identical weather maps from a single source. A newspaper or weather Web site is a good choice. Make sure you write the date on each one as you collect it. And include any needed key to symbols or colors needed to read the map. After a week, order the maps chronologically and compare them. Use the map series to study which way fronts generally move, how long fronts and high and low pressure systems last, and what geographical features (latitude, mountain ranges, sea coast) affect temperatures.

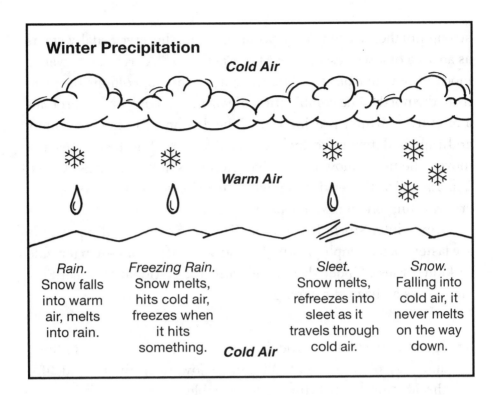

Winter Precipitation

Cold Air

Warm Air

Rain.
Snow falls into warm air, melts into rain.

Freezing Rain.
Snow melts, hits cold air, freezes when it hits something.

Cold Air

Sleet.
Snow melts, refreezes into sleet as it travels through cold air.

Snow.
Falling into cold air, it never melts on the way down.

Winter Storms

Winter storms bring some of the worst weather around. Snow, sleet, freezing rain, fierce winds, and plunging temperatures are all part of winter storms. Many people die each winter from traffic accidents and hypothermia during winter storms. Adding to the misery of winter storms is the fact that they are difficult to forecast. The heaviest snowfalls often occur when the air temperature is hovering around freezing. If the air the snow falls through changes temperature a few degrees one way or the other, the precipitation could end up as rain, sleet, or freezing rain (see diagram above). A mixture of different kinds of precipitation is in fact very likely because the storms that bring snow are often caused by warm fronts sliding over cold air near the ground.

Storm Science

A notorious example is a northeaster, a late fall or winter storm along the Atlantic Coast of North America that brings heavy rain, heavy snow, and coastal flooding. The storm is named for the strong northeast winds they produce. A northeaster usually starts as an area of low pressure near the East Coast. As relatively warm, moist ocean air from the Atlantic surges inland, cold air drops in from the north. The combination of warm and cold air can produce a mixture of winter precipitation. The dividing line between snow and rain is determined by the storm's path. The farther east it moves, the more snow rather than rain falls along the East Coast. The East Coast's heaviest snowfalls usually come from northeasters traveling on an easterly path.

Any winter storm becomes a blizzard if snow is falling, winds are faster than 35 mph (56 km/h), and visibility is one-quarter mile (0.4 km) or less. Under these conditions the National Weather Service issues a blizzard warning.

- A BLIZZARD WARNING advises people in the area to seek refuge and stay off the roads. Blinding snow, deep drifts, and life-threatening temperatures are probable.

- A WINTER STORM WARNING is issued for heavy snow and ice and recommends staying indoors.

- A WINTER STORM WATCH means the conditions exist for the possibility of heavy snow and possible ice and instructs people in the area to prepare now for the storm.

- A WINTER WEATHER ADVISORY indicates that weather conditions could make transportation difficult, but usually not life threatening.

- A FROST/FREEZE WARNING means that below-freezing temperatures are expected and may cause damage to plants. People without heat are advised to seek shelter.

Winter Warnings

Snow doesn't usually kill people. It's other consequences of winter storms that cause deaths. Traffic accidents from poor visibility and slippery road conditions, hypothermia from low temperatures and wind-chill factors, and heart attacks from snow shoveling are the cause of most winter-weather deaths. Fortunately many of the hazards of winter storms can be avoided if you're prepared and use good storm sense.

The National Weather Service (NWS) issues winter warnings, watches, and advisories to assist the public in preparing and dealing with winter weather. Choose one of the five advisories listed on page 122 (blizzard warning, winter storm warning, winter storm watch, winter weather advisory, and frost/freeze warning). Investigate its details, including what it means exactly, when it's issued, and what precautions are recommended. (The storm safety Web sites on page 131 are all good sources of additional information.) Consider making an informational poster that 1) explains the meaning of the advisory, watch, or warning; 2) makes precautionary recommendations; and 3) makes suggestions for being prepared.

El Niño

Weather and the Environment

El Niño is an abnormal warming of the tropical Pacific Ocean that can alter weather around the globe. It's part of the El Niño Southern Oscillation (ENSO), a cycle of changing ocean temperatures, rainfall, atmospheric circulation, vertical motion, and air pressure over the tropical Pacific. An El Niño episode is a warming of the tropical Pacific

Ocean, while a cooling is called a **La Niña**. An El Niño happens every three to four years on average and each lasts from 12 to 18 months. Sometimes a cooling La Niña follows an El Niño, but not always.

What causes an El Niño? A dying down of the trade winds that normally push the top layer of sun-soaked warm ocean water over to the west side of the Pacific ocean. During an El Niño this Pacific ocean pattern of hot on the west side and cool on the east side breaks down. The trade winds slack off and the warm water sloshes away from the west side spreading east. Thunderstorms start to form over the warm shifting water and entire weather patterns in

El Niño / La Niña
TOPEX/POSEIDON and Jason-1

Nov '97

Warm water of
El Niño condition

Feb '99

http://topex-www.jpl.nasa.gov

-18 -14 -10 -6 -2 2 6 10 14 cm
TOPEX/POSEIDON maps of sea surface height relative to normal

Cool water of
La Niña condition

the Pacific are changed as a result. During a strong El Niño, jet streams can be altered and changes in global weather patterns follow. In the United States, for example, El Niño years bring mild winters to the north and rainy ones in the southeast. The west coast waters warm up, while the Rocky Mountains get extra snow.

The ENSO cycle is a natural part of the planet's climate system. It's a way excess heat in the tropics is exported. (Hurricanes are another way.) But although it's natural, an El Niño creates ocean and weather conditions that are not normal. This means floods, droughts, and storms that take a toll on the environment. Wetlands dry up, fires destroy forests, rivers flood, and wildlife and humans are killed and made homeless. Sea life is especially affected. The warmer, less nutrient-rich water during an El Niño means less phytoplankton—the foundation of the sea's food chain that are food for fish and other sea life. The record-setting El Niño of 1997–98 reduced the numbers of sea lions and sea birds and decimated many fish populations.

 Fast Fact

The strong El Niño event of 1982–83 killed more than 2,000 people and caused $13 billion in damage. Scientists have gotten much better at predicting El Niño events since then, thanks to a system of temperature-taking ocean buoys.

Water Warm Up

During an El Niño event, warm ocean water moves eastward. Along with the warm water goes precipitation, so the eastern Pacific gets too much rain while the western is left in drought. Warm water creates more precipitation than cold water because it evaporates more easily. Evaporated water (water vapor) in the air is what condenses into clouds that later falls out as rain. Investigate the connection between water temperature, cloud formation, and rain in this activity.

You'll Need
- ► 2 identical clear jars (glass or plastic)
- ► 2 pieces of heavy-duty aluminum foil (large enough to cover the mouth of the jars)
- ► 2 ice cubes
- ► 2 rubber bands
- ► hot and cold water
- ► grease pencil, permanent marker, or crayon

1. Use a grease pencil, permanent marker, or crayon to label one jar HOT and the other COLD.

2. Fill the HOT jar with hot tap water halfway and the COLD jar to an equal level with cold water.

3. Cover each jar with one of the pieces of foil and secure the foil with rubber bands.

4. At the same time, set an ice cube on top of each jar. Wait about 10 minutes until you see "fog" in one of the jars.

5. Remove the ice cubes. Carefully turn over the pieces of foil and compare what you see. Where did the cloudlike water droplets on the foil come from? Which jar produced more "clouds"?

TV Weather Forecaster

Cool Weather Careers

Gary Amble puts his reputation on the line every morning and noon. He's a meteorologist at KCTV Channel 5 in Kansas City. Every morning and noon he reports the weather and gives a forecast of what's to come. "I think the vast majority of people realize that you're just the messenger," says Amble. But some people do seem to hold him personally responsible for the weather at times, and the weddings or picnics it has ruined. It's all part of being a TV personality. But TV weather forecasters aren't just pretty faces. Most—like Amble—are trained meteorologists recognized by the American Meteorological Society (AMS) with at least a bachelor's degree that includes 20 semester hours of meteorology. "To get your AMS seal [the Society] requires your consecutive weathercasts to be judged by some of your top peers within the Society," explains Amble.

Amble got into meteorology at college through a fondness for other science topics—particularly chemistry. A small cable station in the college town gave him his start in television. Besides being able to turn radar, satellite, and other weather data into a forecast, TV weather forecasters need to be comfortable working on live television. Most forecasters on TV stand in front of what looks like a weather map, but it's actually just a blank wall. They only know where to point by looking at TV screens off camera—kind of like gesturing in a mirror. It can make for confusion. "Unexpected things happen almost every single night," says Amble.

Gathering weather information and making accurate forecasts is just part of television weather forecasters' jobs these days. Most also visit local schools and scout groups, teaching kids about the science behind what they see in the sky and on the TV weather map.

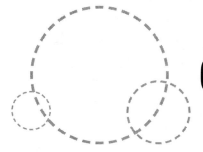

Glossary

acid rain: rain with increased acidity caused by pollutants

air pressure: pressure caused by the weight of the air; atmospheric pressure

atmosphere: the air surrounding Earth or another planet

barometer: an instrument that measures air pressure

cirrus cloud: high wispy cloud usually made of tiny ice crystals

cold front: an advancing edge of a cold air mass

cumulus cloud: fluffy lower cloud that often "grows" on sunny days

El Niño: an irregularly occurring flow of unusually warm surface water along the western coast of South America that disrupts normal weather patterns

gnomon: an object whose shadow indicates the hour of the day on a sundial

greenhouse effect: the warming of the earth's atmosphere that occurs when the sun's radiation passes through the atmosphere, is absorbed by the earth, and is given off as radiation of longer wavelength which can be absorbed by atmospheric gases such as carbon dioxide and water vapor

high pressure system: an area of relative pressure maximum that has outward winds and a rotation opposite to the earth's rotation

La Niña: an irregularly occurring movement of deep cold water to the ocean surface along the western coast of South America, often occurring after an El Niño, that disrupts weather patterns in a manner opposite of an El Niño

latitude: lines on the globe that measure distance from the equator

low pressure system: an area of a relative pressure minimum that has inward winds and rotates in the same direction as the earth

mesocyclone: a rotating column of air inside a thunderstorm

mesosphere: a layer of the atmosphere extending from the top of the stratosphere to an altitude of about 50 miles (80 kilometers)

monsoon: a seasonal wind that blows from the southwest and brings heavy rains

precipitation: the falling of water from clouds in the form of rain, snow, sleet, hail, etc.

stationary front: an air mass that is not moving, or moving very little

stratosphere: an upper portion of the atmosphere above the troposphere where temperature changes little and clouds rarely form

stratus cloud: flat layered low cloud

synoptic chart: a map or chart that shows meteorological or atmospheric conditions over a large area at a given time

thermal inversion: an atmospheric condition in which a layer of warm air settles over a layer of cool air near the ground

tropical depression: a spinning tropical ocean storm in which the surface winds are 38 mph (61 km/h) or less

troposphere: the portion of the atmosphere which extends from the earth's surface to the bottom of the stratosphere and in which temperature generally decreases rapidly with altitude

warm front: an advancing edge of a warm air mass

Weather Web Sites

General Weather Web Sites

American Meteorological Society   www.ametsoc.org/AMS
National Weather Service   www.nws.noaa.gov
USA Today's Weather   www.usatoday.com/weather
The Weather Channel   www.weather.com
Weather Online   www.weatheronline.com
The Weather World 2010 Project   ww2010.atmos.uiuc.edu
World Meteorological Organization   www.wmo.ch

Storm Web Sites

Hurricane Hunters   www.hurricanehunters.com
National Hurricane Center   www.nhc.noaa.gov
National Severe Storms Laboratory   www.nssl.noaa.gov
National Association of Storm Chasers and Spotters:
      www.chasingstorms.com and www.stormchaser.com

Storm Safety Web Sites

American Red Cross   www.redcross.org (click on the "Get Pre-
      pared" tab)
Federal Emergency Management Agency KIDS Homepage
      www.fema.gov/kids

National Weather Service—Weather Safety   www.nws.noaa.gov/
    safety.php

Weather and the Environment Web Sites

Environmental Protection Agency's Acid Rain Program
    www.epa.gov/docs/acidrain
Environmental Protection Agency's Global Warming Site
    www.epa.gov/globalwarming
National Oceanic and Atmospheric Administration's El Niño
    Page   www.elnino.noaa.gov

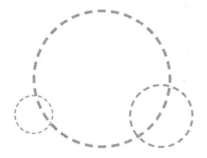

Index